TRICIA A. ZUCKER
& SONIA Q. CABELL

STRIVE-FOR-FIVE

CONVERSATIONS

*A Framework That Gets Kids
Talking to Accelerate Their
Language Comprehension & Literacy*

■SCHOLASTIC

To our children:
Sarah Grace, Anneliese, Virginia, and Joseph.
Thank you for all of the wonderful years
of meaningful, fun conversations!

Senior Vice President and Publisher: Tara Welty
Editorial Director: Sarah Longhi
Development Editor: Raymond Coutu
Senior Editor: Shelley Griffin
Production Editor: Danny Miller
Creative Director: Tannaz Fassihi
Interior Designer: Maria Lilja

CONTENTS

Zucker and Cabell argue convincingly that as children's language expands through conversation, their knowledge does as well. Words are the tip of the iceberg; underlying those words are concepts. As they learn words, children simultaneously acquire, develop, and refine concepts that those words represent. And it is here where you play a crucial role in the learning process.

As this book makes clear, what you do to support conversations has enormous consequences on children's language development, knowledge of their world, and self-confidence in the learning process. Some conversations will be opportunistic, sparked by an event or the realities of classroom life, and not designed to teach something. Yet despite the impromptu nature of those conversations, my research and that of other scholars suggest they are just as informative as conversations you plan. Children not only learn new things from them, but also ways of thinking and problem-solving. They learn the implicit patterns of conversation; expressions, tone, and quality of talk; and "ways of knowing," based on types of questions they're asked and explanations they give.

Other conversations will be more planned and purposeful, as part of your instructional program. As Zucker and Cabell explain in Chapter 3, conversations during read-aloud provide an ideal setting for learning new words in a meaningful context. Couple that with opportunities for children to talk about and use those words, as you scaffold their linguistic and cognitive development, and you'll see their language development and comprehension grow exponentially. This is especially true when you engage children in interesting topics, such as the mysteries of space and the inner workings of machines.

Those kinds of interactions show children how conversations work and give them a "schema" they can use to practice conversations with classmates during free and guided play. That is important because children learn more about language when they hear and use words frequently, in meaningful and playful contexts. For example, studies suggest that conversations during book reading, coupled with opportunities for children to "give it a go" on their own during free and guided play, lead to gains in children's language production and comprehension.

Yet as important as conversations are, it's not always easy to have them with young children. It can be difficult to get a conversation going and keep it flowing. Some children may be shy to talk with adults outside their families. Others may worry about giving a "correct" answer. Others might struggle to find words to capture their ideas. But take heart. This wonderful book will guide your way.

SUSAN B. NEUMAN, Professor, Childhood Education and Literacy Development, New York University

Little Kids Grow...

With Big Conversations

We know that language skills are important for young children. But it can be difficult to engage them in meaningful conversations in busy preschool, kindergarten, and first-grade classrooms. This book's message is simple: You can elevate the quality of your conversations by using the Strive-for-Five framework (Dickinson, 2003; Hadley et al., 2020). What does that mean? Instead of the two- or three-turn conversations that often happen in classrooms...

1. Teacher: What are you drawing?
2. Student: A dog.
3. Teacher: Good job.

...you extend your conversations by striving for five turns:

1. **TEACHER:** What are you drawing?

2. **STUDENT:** A dog.

3. **TEACHER:** Nice. Tell me what made you think about drawing this dog.

4. **STUDENT:** It's my dog. His name is Scout.

5. **TEACHER:** Tell me more about what you like to do with Scout.

In other words, you don't stop after asking students a question and giving them one opportunity to answer. Instead, you keep the conversation going by being responsive to what children are saying and encouraging them to describe their thinking or deepen their knowledge. David Dickinson (2003) pioneered the phrase "strive for five" as a guiding principle to have a sequence of five back-and-forth exchanges with children in conversations.

The early childhood years are perfect for putting children on the road to becoming good conversationalists. Young children not only need routine conversations with their caregivers, but also meaningful ones to develop foundational language skills that prepare them for reading and school success (Dickinson & Porche, 2011; Landry et al., 2021; National Early Literacy Panel, 2008; Neuman, 2006). As students move up the grades, their ability to engage in quality conversations continues to relate to their reading achievement (Goodwin et al., 2021; Sedova et al., 2019).

Conversations are not always easy, particularly for students with limited language skills or multilingual learners. But teachers report that one of the best things about the Strive-for-Five framework is that it enables them to support all children's learning while showing each child that they care about his or her ideas. This is important because children have a deep need to be known and understood by their teachers. By using the Strive-for-Five framework, you show them you want to hear what they have to say.

About This Book

Strive-for-Five Conversations breaks down the art of meaningful conversation for you, busy teachers of young children. We share important research that shows how the quality of classroom conversations influences children's language comprehension and literacy outcomes.

We believe that you can have meaningful conversations when you "strive for five" turns. Specifically, you can:

- Actively listen to what children say to initiate conversations and follow their lead.
- Ask open-ended questions about concrete and abstract ideas to spark meaningful conversations.
- Use scaffolding strategies as you "strive for five" conversation turns about a specific topic.
- Expose young children to a variety of language comprehension goals that align with the science of reading, including:
  - literacy knowledge
  - vocabulary
  - verbal reasoning
  - background knowledge
  - language structures

There are many benefits of stretching conversations with this framework:

- Building trust and strong teacher-student relationships
- Elevating the discourse in your classroom in equitable ways
- Most of all, increasing your students' language comprehension and literacy skills

How This Book Is Organized

Strive-for-Five Conversations is organized into three parts:

PART I is designed to help you understand and implement the Strive-for-Five framework. In Chapter 1, we explain the framework and the importance of starting conversations with open-ended questions and guiding learning by following the child's lead. We encourage you to embrace that method because warm, responsive adults are the kind of people that kids want to talk to! In Chapter 2, we examine the science of reading and why the language comprehension that develops from Strive-for-Five conversations is essential to becoming a skilled reader. In Chapter 3, we address practical ways to weave conversations into your classroom routines. We focus on creating an environment that fosters meaningful, equitable conversation among you and your students, regardless of their cultural and linguistic backgrounds.

PART II digs into how the Strive-for-Five framework allows young children to practice the skills that the science of reading shows are essential to becoming skilled readers. Using Hollis Scarborough's (2001) Reading Rope for inspiration, we consider aspects of language comprehension. In Chapter 4, we focus on the literacy knowledge strand, discussing the genres and qualities of books that promote conversations during interactive reading. In Chapter 5, we zero in on the vocabulary strand, discussing how to use the Strive-for-Five framework to have conversations that build knowledge of new words. In Chapter 6, we focus on ways to encourage children to reason about increasingly complex topics. In Chapter 7, we show you how to build content knowledge over time using the framework. In Chapter 8, we focus on the structures of written language, such as syntax and semantics, which good readers need to comprehend and build knowledge from texts.

PART III shows you how to promote Strive-for-Five conversations at school and home. In Chapter 9, we offer strategies for bringing critical conversation partners to the table: parents and other family members. Families are essential to raising good conversationalists and extending learning at home. Finally, in Chapter 10, we review how to pull together everything we discussed in Chapters 1–9 in ways that add up over time.

Throughout the book, you'll find "Terms to Know" boxes, "Reflect and Implement" questions, and sample conversations to build your knowledge and help you start "striving for five" today!

Conversations Matter for Literacy Development

While developing children's conversational skills is important for many reasons, in this book, we focus on how those skills are foundational to becoming a good reader. At first, it may seem like a stretch to think that conversations can help children learn to read well. But developing oral language (i.e., speaking and listening) through daily conversations is essential for language comprehension and, eventually, reading comprehension (Catts & Petscher, 2022; National Early Literacy Panel, 2008; Silverman et al., 2020). Children begin by listening to texts read aloud and, later, by reading texts on their own. Accumulated research shows that early language predicts later reading comprehension (Hjetland et al., 2020). Indeed, language comprehension is a key part of reading and can be developed from the start of a child's life. And the opposite is true, too: Weaknesses in early language comprehension are tied to later reading difficulties (Petscher et al., 2018). As such, ample opportunities to develop strong language skills are essential for developing good readers (Snowling & Hulme, 2021).

Adults Need Meaningful Conversations, Too!

Although this book focuses on conversations with children, you might find that some of the strategies lead to more meaningful conversations between you and other adults in your life. We humans have a deep need for others to know us (Grusec & Davidov, 2021). In recent years, our increased use of text messaging and social media, as well as our hectic schedules, have made meaningful conversations harder to have (Brown et al., 2016). Don't be afraid to see what happens when you strive for more meaningful conversations inside and outside of the classroom!

A Little About Us and Why We Wrote This Book

We are two former teachers and reading specialists who *love* having extended conversations with children because we never know what they will say! In fact, we have recently had conversations with each other's children, ages 7 and 8, on a variety of topics, ranging from whether Darth Vader is real to why we eat vegetables when we'd much rather eat chocolate. We both taught at Thomas Jefferson Elementary School in Virginia and, during that time, had *many* conversations about how to improve our students' language and literacy skills. We decided to go to graduate school together at the University of Virginia to study language and literacy development and instruction.

When we finished our doctoral program, we realized there were too few easy-to-use resources for preschool, kindergarten, and first-grade teachers on developing language skills. So we started developing and testing new programs to support conversations during whole-group read-alouds and small-group activities. Although that work has helped improve children's vocabulary outcomes (Cabell et al., 2015; Zucker et al., 2019), there is so much more work to do. Teachers need strategies to ensure daily conversations with young children.

We realize that is a big ask! Even for us—as the authors of this book—slowing down, listening to the children and adults in our lives, and engaging in meaningful conversations is hard. Yet our research shows that when educators learn the conversation strategies in this book, they change children's learning trajectories.

So we are excited to share those strategies with you. May they lead to meaningful conversations with your students every day.

(top) Tricia in conversation during a read-aloud

(right) Sonia in conversation during a science investigation

UNDERSTANDING AND IMPLEMENTING THE FRAMEWORK

PART I

CHAPTER 1

Strive for Five

The Art of True Conversation

An impactful conversation—one that advances language skills—can happen with just five turns, or exchanges, between you and your students. Certainly, some conversation topics warrant more turns, but for most topics, just five give children an opportunity to practice meaningful language skills.

Notice how this preschool teacher, Ms. Victoria, pauses for a Strive-for-Five conversation while reading an informational text, *Baby on Board: How Animals Carry Their Young* by Marianne Berkes, about how animals carry their babies. The conversation is about the word *remain*, which appears midway through the book:

1. **MS. VICTORIA:** When someone *remains* somewhere, they stay there. Look at how the mother manatee stays close to her baby. Why do you think she does that?

2. **MICAH:** Cuz she has to stay close.

3. **MS. VICTORIA:** Yes. Why?

4. **MICAH:** So she doesn't get lost.

5. **MS. VICTORIA:** Yes. The baby will be safe if she remains near her momma. The baby won't get lost or go near other animals that might be dangerous.

What a powerful and efficient learning moment! In five conversation turns, Ms. Victoria reinforces the meaning of an important vocabulary word and asks a "why" question to develop Micah's verbal reasoning skills. Then she continues reading to maintain all students' interest in the book.

After reading, Ms. Victoria asks students to consider an important, guiding question. Notice how, in this Strive-for-Five conversation, she supports a student after an ambiguous response to her initial "how" question.

1. **MS. VICTORIA:** We read this story about how animals carry their babies or their offspring. Let's think about today's guiding questions. How are animal parents and human parents the same? Amari, how are animal parents and human parents the same?

2. **AMARI:** Lions eat baby zebras.

3. **MS. VICTORIA:** Yes, lions sometimes eat baby zebras. So how could the momma keep the baby zebra safe?

4. **AMARI:** Hide from the lion.

5. **MS. VICTORIA:** Yes, hiding from the lion could keep the baby zebra safe. Human parents also work hard to keep their babies safe. So, both animal and human parents try to keep their babies safe.

What do you notice about this second conversation? At turn 1, Ms. Victoria helped support all children's attention to the important "guiding question" by stating it again before asking students to answer it. At turn 3, Ms. Victoria followed Amari's lead while eventually getting back to the initial question and modeling a sensible response at her final turn.

Both of those Strive-for-Five conversations contain five turns:

Each of these conversations took about one minute of instructional time, but they accomplished a lot. Strive-for-Five conversations are not happening enough in classrooms (Dickinson, 2003; Early et al., 2010), especially for children experiencing poverty (Neuman et al., 2018a).

Terms to Know

A **Conversation** is a set of back-and-forth verbal messages between two or more speakers on a single topic. When the topic changes, a new conversation starts.

A **Conversation Turn** is marked by a change in speaker. So in a three-turn conversation, a teacher might take a turn, a child might take a turn, and then the teacher might respond by taking another turn.

Intentional Scaffolding is when a teacher's conversation turn guides the child's language and cognitive growth by adding challenge, if the topic is easy for the child to understand, or by simplifying if the topic is challenging. Scaffolds include hints, explanations, models, or follow-up questions.

Language Comprehension is the ability to understand and use language in oral form. When students have strong language skills, they are better able to understand conversations, books read to them, or books they read themselves.

Responsiveness is responding to the child's signals and interests by following the child's lead. This may include responding to what a child says, describing what the child is doing or how he or she is feeling. Adults can respond to positive and negative signals such as, "You are excited to play with that," or "It looks like that is frustrating you."

Research shows that many classroom conversations stop short at the third turn, for example (Cabell et al., 2015; Deshmukh et al., 2022):

1 **TEACHER:** What happened on this page?

2 **STUDENT:** Umm, they are mad.

3 **TEACHER:** Yes, good.

After the third turn, the teacher does not seek another response from the child. In fact, her praise serves as a "conversation stopper." If our goal is to model advanced language that prepares students for reading, we need to have longer, more substantive conversations that contain opportunities for students to push their thinking and model more precise language.

Our research shows that five turns is long enough to elicit a meaningful response but short enough to match most young children's developing attention and language skills.

Let's replay the same conversation using the Strive-for-Five framework. Notice how, in the chart below, the conversation starts with the same open-ended question from the teacher in turn 1, and the same response from the child in turn 2. But, in turn 3, the teacher responds more thoughtfully to what the child said by modeling more precise vocabulary and keeping the conversation going. In turn 4, the student deepens her response. Then the teacher wraps up the conversation in turn 5 by expanding on what the child says by rephrasing or adding more information.

1 TEACHER QUESTION	2 CHILD RESPONDS	3 TEACHER CHALLENGES	4 CHILD RESPONDS	5 TEACHER EXPANDS
What happened on this page?	Umm, they are mad.	Yes, she's very angry. How do you think she should have acted when she got upset?	She should've used her words.	I agree. She could have made a better choice by using words instead of kicking the tower.

Strive-for-Five conversations require a small shift for most of us. To make that shift, rather than asking only one good question, ask a second question to elicit more language from the student. Be sure the question extends the student's thinking about the topic, and doesn't stray to a different topic. By doing that, you pull meaningful language from students *and* show them you're interested in learning more about what they have to say. You build trust because students see that their teacher values their ideas and is interested in keeping the conversation going. In other words, Strive-for-Five conversations say, "I see *you* and hear *you*" because you focus on one student at a time.

Starting a Conversation

Let's first focus on how to open a Strive-for-Five conversation. Did you know that there are dozens of ways to ask questions that elicit a one-word response and far fewer ways to ask them to elicit a multiple-word response? The question form we choose matters when we want to strike up and maintain a conversation with students. All too often well-intentioned teachers ask their students questions such as this:

> **TEACHER:** How are you feeling today?

That lead to responses such as this:

> **STUDENT:** Fine.

And well-intentioned parents ask their children questions such as this:

> **PARENT:** How was your day?

That lead to responses such as this:

> **CHILD:** Okay.

Well, so much for a meaningful conversation! Many educators have been trained to privilege "how" questions because they target higher-order thinking. Although "how" questions are usually good for doing that, only a small subset of them elicit more extended verbal explanation. For example, instead of asking "How is/are/was..." questions that require a one-word answer, consider asking "How can you tell?", or "How do you know?", that requires a multi-word response. Or keep the conversations going after a "How are you feeling?" type of question, using the Strive-for-Five framework.

Ask Open-Ended Questions to Start Conversations

The big goal of this book is to have meaningful, extended conversations with students. So let's consider how to ask open-ended questions that set the stage for those conversations. To understand the power of asking open-ended questions, it might be helpful to discuss their counterpart: closed questions. Closed questions tend to elicit a one-word response from a child (Cabell et al., 2015). How do you know if you're asking an open-ended or closed question? Open-ended questions usually start with adverbs such as *what, where, when,* or *why.* Imagine the types of responses you might get from your students if you use the open-ended question stems in the box below.

Open-ended questions get kids talking because they signal you are curious about their thoughts. On the other hand, closed questions often signal that you're simply checking for understanding.

Types of Questions

An **open-ended question** cannot be adequately answered using just one word. Children will have to use many words to answer the question. An open-ended question may also have several appropriate answers. Open-ended prompts, such as, "Tell me more about...," can work like questions.

A **closed question** can usually be answered with just one word. That's why the most common type of closed question is a yes-or-no question.

Stems That Elicit One-Word and Multi-Word Responses

Closed Question Stems (often a one-word response)	Open-Ended Question Stems (usually a multi-word response)
• How is/are/was...?	• How does this compare to...?
• How many/much...?	• How do you know...?
• Can you...?	• How can you tell what she's feeling?
• Will he...?	• What happened?
• Did you like...?	• What does this remind you of?
• Do you want...?	• Where is the setting of this story?
• Have you been...?	• Who is the kindest character?
• ..., didn't he?	• Which way will they go?
• ..., isn't he?	• Why is she sharing?
• ..., won't he?	• Why do you think that?
• ..., shouldn't he?	
• ..., right?	

We have observed teaching and learning in hundreds of classrooms, and, in our view, effective teachers most often start conversations with open-ended questions (Deshmukh et al., 2019). This is an art form, as those teachers know just the right moments to drop in just the right nice, meaty questions. Some teachers use sticky notes to flag points in books to ask open-ended questions. Others place conversation stems on a poster near each center to remind themselves and students of big ideas that can be investigated there. Yet the single most important thing we observe teachers do after asking an open-ended question is give wait time. Young students need a few seconds to think before they respond, and effective teachers wait for a response before asking another question.

Other Ways to Start Conversations

Although asking open-ended questions is the most common way to start a Strive-for-Five conversation, there are other ways to start them, including:

- asking more about something a child notices.
- joining in play and asking about what the child is doing.
- prompting the child to tell you about an interest or an object she or he is focused on.
- following the child's lead during an unstructured activity.
- making a comment about something she or he is focused on or a problem she or he is trying to solve.

If a child starts a conversation, it might look like this...

And it might sound like this...

1 **STUDENT:** Look at mine.

2 **TEACHER:** What can you tell me about your picture?

3 **STUDENT:** This is me and my sister.

4 **TEACHER:** You and your sister, Emilia, are wearing colorful dresses. What story were you thinking of when you drew this?

5 **STUDENT:** We went to church and played on the playground.

6 **TEACHER:** Nice. I wonder if you could draw more of the setting to show the playground and where it is at church. Then you might add a title.

Be flexible when it comes to starting conversations with students because sometimes thoughtful comments can spark conversations also, such as, "I notice you painted with many colors today!" In Chapter 8, we consider how your responses to children's messages have a huge impact on developing their language skills (Barnes et al., 2021).

Give Wait Time

Open-ended questions are so important to Strive-for-Five conversations! Some preschool teachers immediately follow open-ended questions with closed questions, without giving children a chance to adequately answer the open-ended questions (Wasik & Hindman, 2011a). This can be easy to do! But we want children to think and respond, and that requires wait time.

Deciding to Step It Up or Step It Down: The Scaffolding Ladder

Asking an open-ended question is the first teacher turn in a Strive-for-Five conversation. But the exchange really unfolds with his or her next turn—the teacher scaffold.

The third conversation turn is pivotal because you guide children's learning using scaffolding strategies: hints, models, explanations, or other moves. Scaffolding strategies should be selected to match students' level of understanding at a particular moment in the conversation. You must decide whether to step it up to add challenge to the conversation or step it down to provide support. Use the upward and downward scaffolding strategies listed in the box on the following page (Deshmukh et al., 2022).

The Scaffolding Ladder

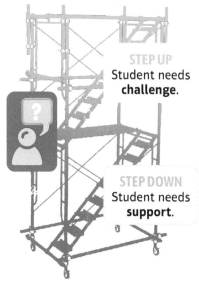

STEP UP
Student needs **challenge**.

STEP DOWN
Student needs **support**.

UPWARD SCAFFOLDING STRATEGIES

- Ask the student to explain reasoning, thinking, feelings, or abstract ideas.
- Push the student to look for patterns or generalize.
- Challenge the student to consider alternatives.
- Extend or add information to the student's idea.

DOWNWARD SCAFFOLDING STRATEGIES

- Reframe or simplify your question.
- Offer the student respectful, corrective feedback.
- Recast the student's response by modeling formal syntax and grammar.
- Give the student a fill-in-the blank response.
- Model the answer and ask the student to repeat it.

At the third turn, you must decide if you will step things up a notch or step them down. We refer to that decision as upward or downward scaffolding to meet learners where they are. That requires listening to the student's response and deciding if it is correct or not.

> *Correct/clear responses* that call for an **upward scaffold** are in keeping with the conversation topic. They are also supported by facts and evidence in situations where you're checking understanding of information you're discussing or in a book you're reading aloud.

> *Incorrect/unclear responses* that call for a **downward scaffold** may be factually incorrect, partially correct, or ambiguous.

When a student offers an appropriate response, then it is your turn to step it up—or increase the demand of the conversation—with an upward scaffold. When your students give incorrect or unclear responses, then it is time to offer support. Guide the child's learning by stepping it down or simplifying the demand of the conversation with a downward scaffold.

The great news is that this is intuitive to most early childhood teachers! Research shows that teachers are skilled in knowing how to respond to children to match their needs. They tend to match children's incorrect responses with downward scaffolds and their correct responses with upward scaffolds almost perfectly (Deshmukh et al., 2022).

However, during whole-group, interactive read-alouds, most teachers scaffold children's responses only about half the time, which is unfortunate because read-aloud is an ideal context to provide language support. Take time during every read-aloud to stretch some conversations using scaffolding strategies. Remember, high-quality conversations with students are linked to better language skills (Cabell et al., 2015; Romeo et al., 2018). With the small pivot to Strive-for-Five conversations, you make a big difference in your students' language skills and eventual reading achievement.

What Matters Most? The Quality of Conversations or Quantity of Words?

To build healthy language functions in the brain, conversation turns are more important than the sheer number of words young children hear, according to a study by Romeo and colleagues (2018), which included 36 children ages 4- to 6-years-old, from diverse socioeconomic backgrounds. The researchers asked children to listen to stories while getting brain scans (i.e., functional magnetic resonance imaging [fMRI]). They also asked children to wear a recording device with their parents over the weekend. Then the researchers looked at relations between the home language environment, brain function, and standardized language measures.

The results are incredible for two reasons. First, children who had more conversations with their caregivers had stronger brain functions for comprehending language. Second, conversation turns benefited kids from all socioeconomic backgrounds. That is, increasing conversation turns reduced initial disparities in vocabulary skills between students who were experiencing poverty and students who were not. The results point to the need for Strive-for-Five conversations at home and school because they can level the playing field for all children, regardless of economic background.

Use Scaffolding Strategies to Challenge and Support

When you know in which direction you need to move on the scaffolding ladder, how do you choose a scaffolding strategy? There's a range of hints, explanations, and supports to use to enhance young children's learning (Cabell et al., 2013; Pentimonti & Justice, 2010). You want to select a strategy that provides just the right level of support for the student's current level of understanding. Minimize the student's dependence on you by offering the minimum amount of support necessary (Vygotsky, 1978).

For example, when a child needs a downward scaffold, you want to simplify the conversation. You want to reduce the complexity and alleviate any stress the child may be feeling. Think of downward scaffolds along a continuum from those that provide minimal, moderate, and intense levels of support (van Kleeck et al., 2003).

Watch downward scaffolding strategies during Strive-for-Five conversations.

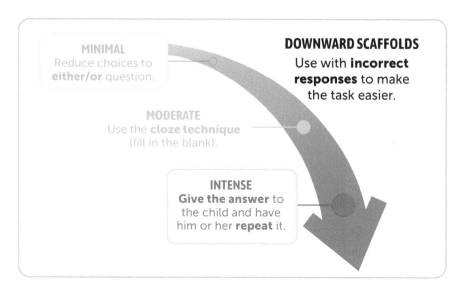

MINIMAL
Reduce choices to **either/or** question.

MODERATE
Use the **cloze technique** (fill in the blank).

INTENSE
Give the answer to the child and have him or her **repeat** it.

DOWNWARD SCAFFOLDS
Use with **incorrect responses** to make the task easier.

Start at the "minimal" level and see if that leads to success. If not, keep stepping down the ladder and offering moderate or even intensive support until you elicit a verbal response from the child. The chart on the next page provides tools to elicit at least a one-word verbal response from almost all students (Zucker et al., 2019).

Downward Scaffolding Strategies

Support Level	Scaffold Type	What You Do	Example
MINIMAL	**Reframe Question**	Reframe the original question to an easier question, an either/or question, or a question with limited response options.	T: What is happening? S: She… T: Is she sharing?
	Give Visual Hints	Point to picture clues or visual reminders to support recall or understanding.	T: What's this? S: (No response) T: It is one of our vocabulary words (points to picture card)
	Recast	Restate the child's answer modeling formal syntax or grammar.	S: I goed to the park. T: You went to the park.
MODERATE	**Cloze or Co-Participating**	Use a fill-in-the-blank or cloze technique with rising intonation that implies the child should complete the sentence with a word or phrase. Or encourage the child to produce a correct response by doing it together with the teacher or a peer.	T: She decided to let him… S: Pick T: Yes! She let him pick the toy.
INTENSE	**Model and Repeat**	Provide an exact model and prompt the child to repeat the correct response.	S: They messing up the building T: Castle. Can you say *castle*? S: Yeah, castle

Likewise, when a student needs an upward scaffold, push for higher-level conversations without stretching too far beyond the student's abilities.

Upward scaffolds range from requiring just a bit of challenge to requiring complex cognitive skills and reasoning (van Kleeck et al., 2003). They fall on a continuum from minimal to intense challenge, taking into account thinking and language required for the student to keep the conversation going.

Watch upward scaffolding strategies during Strive-for-Five conversations.

a fence?"). When you strive for five turns, be confident in knowing you're having meaningful, high-quality exchanges that are just long enough to maintain children's attention. Part of your role as a responsive conversation partner is to read a child's signals as you read the room. You can then decide if you need to wrap up the conversation to keep the flow of an activity, such as a read-aloud, moving.

In an informal space, such as a center or the playground, you might be able to strive for six or more conversation turns, scaffolding upward or downward to match the child's language. Regardless of the situation, maintain the child's attention and stick to the topic. Below is an example of a Strive-for-Five conversation using a downward scaffolding strategy.

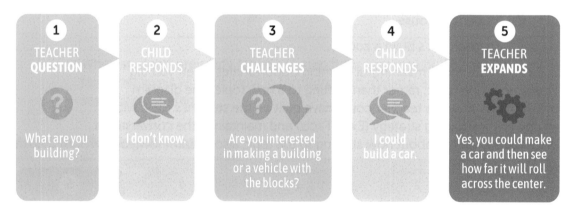

Where to Strike Up Strive-for-Five Conversations

Who are the people in your life that you most enjoy talking with? Are there ways they extend meaningful conversations that you want to bring to your Strive-for-Five approach? In many ways, becoming a good conversationalist is an art form without a single approach. Intentional conversations can happen at any of those times, in formal and informal learning contexts of early childhood classrooms (Barnes et al., 2021; Neuman & Knapczyk, 2022).

Formal situations include interactive read-alouds, circle time, whole- or small-group time, and individual play at centers or workstations. Informal situations include meal or snack times, transition times, and outdoor play or recess.

- Meal or snack times
- Transition times (e.g., arrival/dismissal, handwashing)
- Outdoor play or recess

Reflect on the types of questions you ask in your classroom and other settings that lend themselves to back-and-forth conversations.

For many teachers, interactive read-alouds is the easiest formal situation to practice Strive-for-Five conversations initially, and meal or snack time can be the easiest informal situation. Consider using the open-ended conversations starters in the box below, which can fuel your Strive-for-Five conversations in formal and informal classroom situations.

Conversations Starters for Formal and Informal Classroom Situations

Formal Situations	Informal Situations
• What does it mean to feel frustrated/jealous/etc.?	• Would you rather get a hug or a high five from a friend? Why?
• What does it mean to feel empathy/guilty/etc.?	• What makes your family special?
• What is the hardest thing about…growing up/changing/trying new things/etc.?	• Describe your family members.
• What things scare/worry you? Do you think you should be afraid of these things or are they not a problem?	• What chores and responsibilities do you have at home?
• When friends get upset with one another, it can be hard. What can you do to solve problems with friends?	• Would you rather help with dishes or laundry? Why?
• Sometimes we make poor choices/get into arguments/etc. What is something you could do next time to prevent that?	• Describe a food you didn't used to like but now you do.
• It can be hard to stand up for something you think is right. How can you be strong enough to stand up for the right thing?	• What's one food you like to eat when you're feeling sick?
	• What are your favorite games to play?
	• How do you feel when you have to share toys? Which toys are most fun to share?
	• What are your favorite movies?
	• Who are three movie characters you'd like to share a meal with?
	• What would you rather do: Draw, read, or sing?

Final Word: Grow Language With Just Five Conversation Turns

Strive-for-Five conversations are important for developing the language comprehension of children in your class. We recommend initiating conversations with open-ended questions that help children to think and answer with more than a one-word response. Then, based on the child's response, the teacher scaffolds upward or downward to meet his or her needs. At the same time, the teacher encourages the conversation to continue. These conversations can take place in many contexts across the day, but the interactive read-aloud context provides an important opportunity to talk about learning. In the next chapter, we dig into how Strive-for-Five conversations fit into the research related to the science of reading.

Reflect and Implement

- What did you learn in this chapter that confirms or contradicts how you engage children in conversation?

- Think about your conversations with children. Where do you usually have them? How many turns do your conversations with children typically have? Do they contain just three turns or the goal of five turns?

- What classroom conditions make it easier or harder for you to keep conversations going?

- What upward and downward scaffolds do you tend to use? Are there minimal, moderate, or intense scaffolds you may use with certain students?

Language Comprehension...

and the Science of Reading

Cameron listens to his kindergarten teacher, Mr. Jimenez, read aloud *Why Do Animals Hibernate?* by David Martin, using the knowledge he already has about hibernation to help him learn new information about it. He learns some new vocabulary words and deepens his understanding of other words. He is also hearing the complex language structures used in written language that are too difficult for him to read on his own. The informational text helps him to also understand features of the text genre as Mr. Jimenez draws attention to them, such as how a table of contents works. After reading the book aloud,

Mr. Jimenez repeats the open-ended question he asked students to think about while he was reading, "Why do animals hibernate?" This question challenges students to think beyond the here and now and make inferences.

1 MR. JIMENEZ: Why do animals hibernate?

2 CAMERON: They want to get away during the winter.

3 MR. JIMENEZ: Why do you think they want to get away during the winter?

4 CAMERON: They don't have food.

5 MR. JIMENEZ: Yes, some animals hibernate because food is hard to find during the winter. So they eat a lot when food is available and then go into a long, deep sleep when food is scarce.

Terms to Know

Background Knowledge is the information a reader or listener has about topics in the text. It also includes the information that a person brings into conversations.

Formal Language is the language of written texts used in school that is academic, with more complex language structures.

Informal Language is the language we use in everyday conversations and interactions.

Language Structures refers to how we combine words to craft sentences, including grammatical rules (e.g., syntax) and how word choice affects meaning (e.g., semantics).

Literacy Knowledge is understanding how books and print work to include familiarity with diverse genres, text structures, and text features, as well as how to use these materials for different purposes.

The Reading Rope is a graphic representation of the skills that underlie word recognition and language comprehension, created by researcher Hollis Scarborough (2001).

The Science of Reading is an ever-evolving body of research on how children learn to read. It includes well-established frameworks, theories, and empirical studies on what works to build children's language and literacy skills.

The Simple View of Reading is an equation that describes skilled reading, with reading comprehension being the product of decoding and language comprehension ($D \times C = R$), first posited by Philip Gough and William Tunmer (1986).

Verbal Reasoning is using language to explain ideas aloud or think about and learn new information.

Vocabulary is all the words we know and use. It is also referred to as our *lexicon*.

As we strive for five turns in our conversations with our students, we support language comprehension in the earliest grades. We both strengthen their comprehension of texts now and set the stage for comprehending later, when they're reading complex texts on their own, whether they're trying to learn something new or escaping into a story (Castles et al., 2018). And reading comprehension—or reading for understanding—is our ultimate goal. But for that to happen, children need to start developing important skills early in life.

Models of Reading

Before we unpack language comprehension, let's turn our attention to research on how children learn to read—or, you might say, the *science of reading*. The science of reading is not a narrow, fixed set of knowledge. Rather, it's well-established frameworks, theories, and studies on what works to build language and literacy skills. The science is ever accumulating and evolving as research uncovers new insights and confirms (or debunks) existing ideas about how literacy develops (Petscher et al., 2020).

Two models help to explain the components of reading: the Simple View of Reading and the Reading Rope. Both of them showcase the important role of language comprehension.

The Simple View of Reading

The Simple View is an equation that describes skilled reading. Reading comprehension (R) is the product of decoding (D) and language comprehension (C) (Gough & Tunmer, 1986; Hoover & Tunmer, 2018).

$$D \times C = R$$

Decoding (D) is the ability to map the letters of the alphabet to the sounds of spoken language. As students learn to do that, they begin to recognize words more quickly as they encounter them in text (Ehri, 2005). That is why the D has also been labeled "word recognition."

Language comprehension (C) is the ability to understand what we read or what is read to us, such as during a read-aloud, and what is said to us, such as during a Strive-for-Five conversation.

Decoding (D) and language comprehension (C) are essential to understanding what we read (R). If either component is missing (that is, a zero in the equation), skilled reading is impossible. If either one is compromised, reading is difficult.

The Reading Rope

The Reading Rope (Scarborough, 2001) is a graphic representation of the skills that underlie word recognition and language comprehension—skills that children use more strategically and automatically as their reading develops.

The Simple View emphasizes the two categories of skills required for reading comprehension, while the Reading Rope digs into the specific interwoven skills we must teach children for them to become successful readers.

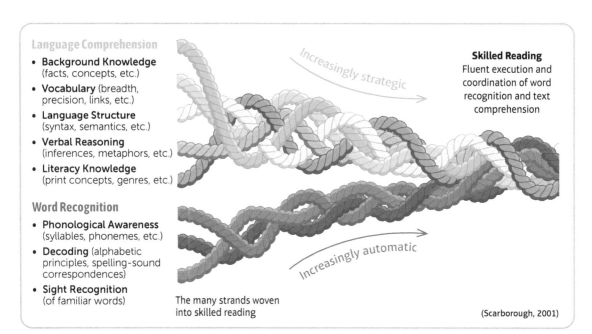

Language Comprehension

- **Background Knowledge** (facts, concepts, etc.)
- **Vocabulary** (breadth, precision, links, etc.)
- **Language Structure** (syntax, semantics, etc.)
- **Verbal Reasoning** (inferences, metaphors, etc.)
- **Literacy Knowledge** (print concepts, genres, etc.)

Word Recognition

- **Phonological Awareness** (syllables, phonemes, etc.)
- **Decoding** (alphabetic principles, spelling-sound correspondences)
- **Sight Recognition** (of familiar words)

Increasingly strategic

Skilled Reading
Fluent execution and coordination of word recognition and text comprehension

Increasingly automatic

The many strands woven into skilled reading

(Scarborough, 2001)

Early Literacy Skills to Lay the Groundwork for Later Reading

The skills that underlie reading start developing early for most children, before formal schooling begins (Whitehurst & Lonigan, 1998). For word recognition, those skills include identifying letter names and sounds (alphabet knowledge) and recognizing the sounds in spoken language (phonological awareness). The underpinnings of language comprehension include oral language and knowledge.

Early in development, those skills are highly related (Storch & Whitehurst, 2002). Take vocabulary, for example. Developing a store of words, or a *lexicon*, helps students decode those words when they encounter them in text (Duke & Cartwright, 2021). Think about the word *purpose*. If a student isn't familiar with that word in spoken language, how can the student accurately decode it when he or she encounters it in text? It could be easily confused with the word *porpoise*. Developing a large lexicon may also build young children's phonological awareness (Metsala & Walley, 1998).

As children move through the elementary grades, and they begin to recognize words more automatically, they increasingly rely on language comprehension, specifically background knowledge, vocabulary, language structures, verbal reasoning, and literacy knowledge (LARRC, 2015). Be sure to develop children's language comprehension alongside their word recognition because it takes time to build. The chapters that follow will help you do that.

Informal and Formal Language Impact Language Comprehension

Young children learn spoken language mainly through daily verbal interactions with the people around them—or *informal language*. In the process, they learn words and concepts, as well as syntax—or language structures. Their understanding of words and concepts deepens when those daily verbal interactions occur over time, on an ongoing basis.

Informal language is important to developing language comprehension, but children also need exposure to *formal language*, the more academic language of school and most texts (Foorman et al., 2016). When you read aloud to students, for example, they begin to learn the common vocabulary and language structures of texts.

That vocabulary and those language structures aren't typically used in everyday conversations. A book we might read to preschoolers typically contains more advanced vocabulary than a conversation between college-educated adults (Cunningham & Stanovich, 1998). And the conversations children have at home can be quite different from the ones they have at school. For example, consider the following informal conversation between a mother and Trey, her six-year-old son, at a restaurant:

1 MOTHER: What side do you want?

2 TREY: French fries!

3 MOTHER: No, we need something healthier than that. How about a vegetable?

4 TREY: French fries?

5 MOTHER: No, choose between broccoli and carrots.

Next, consider this more formal conversation between Trey and his teacher during lunch (adapted with permission from Barnes, Grifenhagen, & Dickinson, 2020):

1 TEACHER: What vegetables do you have on your plate?

2 TREY: Apples!

3 TEACHER: An apple is a fruit. I wonder what kind of vegetables you have.

4 TREY: Broccoli.

5 TEACHER: I see broccoli and green beans on your plate. Both are vegetables and both are healthy for you because they help your body have the nutrients it needs to grow strong.

Now consider another conversation that Trey has at school, after a read-aloud of a book about Asia:

1. **TEACHER:** What are some things we learned about Asia from reading this book?

2. **TREY:** Three out of every five people on Earth lives there!

3. **TEACHER:** Yes, about 60% of the world's population lives on the continent of Asia.

4. **TREY:** Yeah, and it's big. Russia is the biggest!

5. **TEACHER:** Russia is the largest country in Asia and in the whole world, in terms of land area. Part of Russia is also in Europe.

6. **TEACHER:** (starting a new Strive-for-Five conversation with another student) Tracy, what are some other countries in Asia that have large numbers of people or amounts of land?

Those three examples tell us a lot about how conversations at home and school differ. School conversations usually focus on topics under study and contain advanced vocabulary (for example, *population*, *continent*) and standard grammar. Informal conversations contain interpersonal cues so participants do not have to be as specific. For example, Trey could infer, because he and his mother were reading a menu, that she meant what side dish did he want with his dinner, not another meaning, such as: Do you want to sit on the left or right side?

In contrast, Trey's teacher knows that the language of learning at school needs to be more precise. That's why in turn 5 she uses specific details to extend what Trey is saying. Read-alouds and other instructional times of the day encourage the use of more formal language. In this way, you'll grow children's content knowledge and expose them to advanced language models (Cabell, DeCoster, et al., 2013). To accelerate the language comprehension needed for later reading comprehension, we need to not only have *more* conversations with students, but also conversations that will nurture and nourish their formal language.

The Strands of Language Comprehension

Here, we define strands from Scarborough's Reading Rope that comprise language comprehension, and what research says about each one. In Part II, we show you how to use Strive-for-Five conversations to build young children's skills in each strand.

Literacy Knowledge

Literacy knowledge includes understanding the features and structures of different kinds of texts. To build literacy knowledge, expose students to a variety of genres, including narrative and informational texts, early and often.

Different genres elicit different types of conversations between teachers and children. For example, informational texts—texts that convey factual information or describe how to do something—have been increasingly emphasized in standards. The Common Core State Standards (National Governor's Association, 2010) recommend that about 50% of texts read aloud in the primary grades be informational. Informational texts lead to conversations that contain more formal language (Price et al., 2012; Zucker et al., 2010). They also impact children's content knowledge development (Wang et al., 2023). Chapter 4 explains how to select high-quality books for read-alouds and Chapter 7 gives examples of curated sets of texts to build knowledge.

Vocabulary

Vocabulary is the bank of words that we know and use to communicate. *Receptive vocabulary* includes the words we can understand when listening or reading. *Expressive vocabulary* includes the words that we use when speaking or writing.

Vocabulary is a robust predictor of reading comprehension (National Early Literacy Panel, 2008; Ricketts et al., 2007). The more words students know, and the better they know them, the more likely they will be able to understand what they read. Cognitive scientists theorize that we organize vocabulary into networks of knowledge (Willingham, 2006) to represent what we know about the natural and social worlds (Anderson & Nagy, 1993). Some estimate that young children need to learn 1,000–4,000 words per year (Biemiller, 2010; Snow & Kim, 2007). Chapter 5 explains how to teach vocabulary explicitly and how to choose words that are worth teaching.

Verbal Reasoning

Verbal reasoning is thinking and using words to advance our understanding. We use verbal reasoning to make sense of what we read or hear. A big piece of that is understanding abstract concepts by making inferences, or forming a logical conclusion based on reasoning. Strong readers and listeners make inferences about a text as it unfolds. Writers and speakers don't generally include all the information one must know to understand their message—if they did, it would be quite tedious. Rather, the writer/speaker assumes the reader/listener has background knowledge to understand the general message and fill in gaps. For example, Tricia recently said to her children, "The pool man broke the light. We can't let Rosie out." Well, to understand those statements, the children would have to infer that the accident might have resulted in shards of glass near the pool area, and that Rosie (the dog) shouldn't be let out of the house until it is cleaned up, because she might cut her paws.

Inferring has been referred to as the "cornerstone of comprehension" (Orcutt et al., 2023). When someone makes an inference, they activate background knowledge. Then they integrate that knowledge with the new information that they are receiving to make sense of it. In Chapter 6, we discuss how you can foster inferring and abstract thinking by asking students questions during interactive read-alouds.

Background Knowledge

Background knowledge is the information a reader or listener has about topics in the text. Students in the upper grades need background knowledge in science and social studies (e.g., knowledge of the natural and social world) to understand much of what they are expected to read. Building background knowledge should start in preschool.

Background knowledge is essential to helping a reader or listener make inferences about a text. It also includes the information that a person brings into conversations. It is not surprising that the knowledge we have about a text's topic is a key factor in determining whether we understand that text (Anderson & Pearson, 1984). Readers and listeners integrate their background knowledge with the text not only to understand it, but also to learn from it. Chapter 7 addresses systematic ways to build knowledge over time.

Language Structures

Language structures refer to how we combine words to craft sentences, including grammatical rules (e.g., syntax, verb tenses) and how word choice affects meaning (e.g., semantics). These structures matter for understanding written and spoken language. Exposure to written language early on is essential because the language structures of books are often different and more complex than those of spoken language.

Teacher talk—and the level of sophistication of that talk—affects students' understanding. There is a direct connection between the syntactic complexity of what teachers say and how well students can understand formal language. When preschool teachers use formal language structures in their talk, students' understanding of these structures increases (Huttenlocher et al., 2002). The Strive-for-Five framework is focused on modeling and eliciting formal and mature language structures. Chapter 8 shows how to use the framework to model formal language structures by recasting and extending what students say.

Language Comprehension Is a "Long Game"

Much of early reading and writing instruction is—and should be—devoted to *phonics*, the practice of mapping letters or groups of letters (graphemes) onto individual sounds (phonemes), to help children become automatic decoders and recognize many words. But we can't stop there!

We must also develop language comprehension by engaging students in Strive-for-Five conversations across the day, which exposes them to formal language structures and builds their knowledge. Teachers often miss that opportunity because they may not immediately see the difference that developing language comprehension makes. To make matters more complicated, we can't easily measure growth in language comprehension using common classroom assessment tools.

It takes time to build an understanding of the various forms of spoken and written language (Neuman, 2006; Snow, 1991). When students are around 10 years old, in fourth or fifth grade, the effect of language skills on reading increases, while the effect of decoding skills decreases (LARRC, 2015). Developing language comprehension is a long game like many other aspects of life, such as maintaining your health and investing for your retirement. One workout won't transform your abs to a six-pack. You have to save diligently, over time, to be able to retire comfortably. Developing students' language comprehension is the same—you have to make small investments daily to build the constellation of language skills students need to succeed in school, college, and in their careers. By strengthening the language comprehension of PreK, kindergarten, and first-grade students, you prevent later reading difficulties (Hjetland et al., 2020).

Consider that by fourth grade, students will need to read and understand a passage such as this one from *All About Rocks: Discovering the World Beneath Your Feet* by Alessandra Potenza (2021):

> Look closely at a rock and you'll notice chunks and streaks of different colors and sizes. These are the minerals that make up the rock. There are more than 5,000 minerals on Earth. But about 90 percent of the rocks in Earth's crust are made of just one group of minerals: silicates. Silicates include the most abundant elements found in the crust: oxygen and silicon. These elements were created inside stars!

To understand this passage, readers need to use their language comprehension. Regarding literacy knowledge, familiarity with informational texts helps students understand how this genre works. Students must be somewhat familiar with the vocabulary, including words such as *minerals*, *elements*, and *silicon*. In addition to vocabulary, students must use verbal reasoning to infer that, according to scientists, the different colors that exist in rocks come from different minerals. Background knowledge about rocks and minerals would also help with that inference, as students better understand what the rocks in Earth's crust are made of and where they came from. Students must also be able to understand the sentence's language structure. For example, they must understand that the words following a colon describe the earlier part of the sentence and can include a list.

There is a lot that goes into understanding a simple passage about rocks in Earth's crust! So accelerating students' language comprehension in the early grades can make a difference in learning later on.

Multilingual Learners Need Formal Language Support

If you teach multilingual learners, you may notice them speaking English fluently on the playground, but not during interactive read-alouds, writing, formal assessments, and other situations that require expressing complex ideas. This may be due to the challenges and demands of formal-language use in mainstream American English, such as addressing abstract topics and using advanced vocabulary and grammatical structures. In contrast, the informal language they use on the playground includes more gestures, visual cues, or other contextual supports, as well as basic vocabulary and grammatical structures. Multilingual learners usually master informal language earlier than formal language (Cummins, 2012, 2013).

You play a key role in helping young multilingual learners build the formal language skills they need to succeed in school. In middle school, multilingual learners can struggle with reading comprehension if they have not been given sufficient opportunities in elementary school to develop formal

Help All Students Succeed

Around 7.5% of students experience Developmental Language Disorder (DLD) (Hendricks et al., 2019), which is associated with reading difficulties (Catts & Petscher, 2022), and need intensive language support.

But there are also many students without DLD or related clinical disorders who still experience language difficulties. It's important to assess language skills early on to identify those students so they are not overlooked.

A Multi-Tiered System of Support (MTSS) framework benefits students who exhibit low language (Zucker et al., 2021). Students receive increasingly intensive tiers of support based on their needs. Coyne et al. (2022) reported that an MTSS framework can accelerate vocabulary learning for students with low language when they received supplemental small-group instruction in addition to whole-class instruction.

If you are providing higher tiers of language support to a child and they are not making gains or if there is persistent parental concern about their child's language or other skills, work to refer the child for a more formal language evaluation. Diagnostic services are available through school districts and various local early intervention services.

language (Kieffer & Lesaux, 2010). In the remaining chapters, we show you how to do that by engaging multilingual children in intentional, Strive-for-Five conversations, as well as these other research-based strategies (Larson et al., 2020):

- Interactive read-alouds with open-ended questions
- Explicit instruction, such as teaching vocabulary using visual supports
- Instructional adaptations, such as selectively translating words or phrases, to bridge English and children's home languages

You are also critical to helping families of young multilingual learners understand the value of maintaining their home language. There are many benefits to speaking multiple languages, including cultural, economic, and perhaps cognitive advantages (Blanc et al., 2022; van den Noort et al., 2019). As multilingual learners enter U.S. schools, they may focus on speaking English. However, in Chapter 9, we consider how educators who view multilingualism as a strength can help children and parents understand that it is valuable to maintain and build children's home language(s).

Final Word: Strive for Five to Embrace the Science of Reading

Developing language comprehension early in students' school careers is essential to supporting their overall reading and writing development. We must provide students frequent opportunities to hear and use formal language. Using Scarborough's Reading Rope as a framework for Part II, we focus on ways to accelerate young children's language comprehension by engaging them in Strive-for-Five conversations—conversations that focus on a single topic for multiple turns and build on what students say. Those conversations also give you the opportunity to model advanced vocabulary and syntax, help students to think abstractly, and build their knowledge of the social and natural world.

Reflect and Implement

How does information in this chapter fit with your existing knowledge of the science of reading? In which areas do you want to deepen your understanding of the science of reading in practice?

How does your current practice facilitate language comprehension growth?

Do you feel that your classroom has a balance of informal and formal conversations? In what contexts do you notice each type happening?

How can Strive-for-Five conversations help students better understand formal language?

CHAPTER 3

Creating Classroom Routines...

for Strive-for-Five Conversations

In one of the largest studies of state-funded PreK, the National Center for Early Development and Learning found that teachers and children were engaged in conversation for only 6% of the school day (Early et al., 2010). How can you create routines in your classroom that ensure and support ongoing Strive-for-Five conversations? This chapter answers that question. We consider daily decisions and situations that create space for engaging conversations. Chances are, you already have routines for promoting conversations during read-alouds (Dickinson & Smith, 1994). The routines suggested in this chapter will enhance your read-alouds and other points in the day in which you and children connect.

How Good Conversation Habits Become Routine

Teachers make hundreds, even thousands, of decisions each day. Making in-the-moment decisions *while* teaching is sometimes called the "heart of teaching" (Bishop, 2008). You often have little time to make a decision during the flow of a lesson or activity. A key moment is when you decide whether to stretch the conversation to scaffold learning or steer it onto the next topic (Dickinson & Smith, 1994; Molinari et al., 2013; Myhill & Warren, 2005).

When you embrace the Strive-for-Five framework, you embrace a "conversations count" mindset, meaning you commit to listening to children and keeping conversations with them going when possible. You may already have that mindset. Or it may seem like it requires a lot of effort to achieve it and, indeed, it may at first. But once you have achieved it, Strive-for-Five conversations become easier and an excellent way to elicit students' language and perspectives. Teachers who engage children in Strive-for-Five

Terms to Know

Center Time gives students choices of how to work or play independently or with peers, as they practice skills or do activities you have introduced.

Conversations Count Mindset means being committed to listening actively and keeping conversations going.

Equity Sticks are tools for calling on students—simple popsicle sticks with students' names on them—that signal it is one child's turn to have a conversation with the teacher.

Free Play is a totally child-directed activity time when children explore materials or draw and create on their own.

Guided Play is a time when children direct the play activities while adults scaffold their language, cognitive, and social development.

Interactive Read-Aloud is a whole-group or small-group activity in which the teacher reads aloud a book and discusses it with students.

A **Peer Conversation** is a child-managed activity that involves two to five students engaged in discussion during the school day.

Pragmatic Language Skills are the abilities to use formal and informal language appropriately in social situations. The emphasis is not just on what you say, but how you say it.

Small-Group Language Activities are teacher-managed activities that allow two to five children time to more deeply understand concepts or to practice using new vocabulary and more complex sentences.

Turn and Talk is a routine that signals to students to have a conversation with a peer.

conversations provide more effective vocabulary instruction during interactive read-alouds, which require dozens of decisions about when to pause and discuss the text, without losing its flow and meaning (Zucker et al., 2023). We have also found that as Strive-for-Five conversations become a regular routine, they become a good habit rather than a conscious decision (Zucker et al., 2020).

Your initial Strive-for-Five conversations may require you to make in-the-moment decisions—that is, to decide whether to have a shorter, more typical conversation made up of three turns, with a teacher question, student response, teacher praise—or a longer one with at least five turns (Deshmukh et al., 2022; Wasik et al., 2022). The chart below outlines the decision-making process when engaged in a conversation with a student.

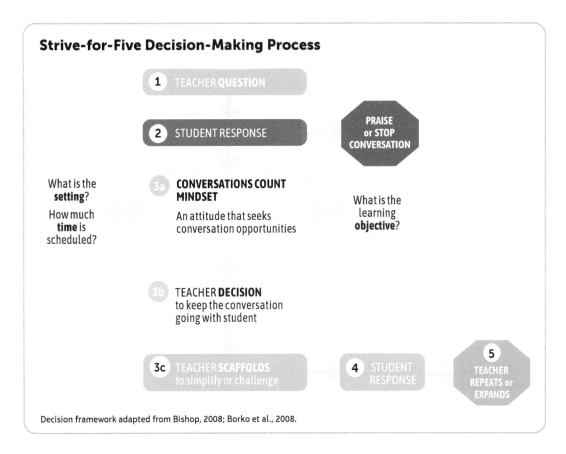

Strive-for-Five Decision-Making Process

1 TEACHER **QUESTION**

2 STUDENT RESPONSE

PRAISE or STOP CONVERSATION

What is the **setting**?

How much **time** is scheduled?

3a **CONVERSATIONS COUNT MINDSET**
An attitude that seeks conversation opportunities

What is the learning **objective**?

3b **TEACHER DECISION**
to keep the conversation going with student

3c TEACHER **SCAFFOLDS** to simplify or challenge

4 STUDENT RESPONSE

5 TEACHER REPEATS or EXPANDS

Decision framework adapted from Bishop, 2008; Borko et al., 2008.

Why does all this matter? These types of extended conversations in early childhood classrooms offer opportunities for feedback and build knowledge while modeling advanced language (Cabell et al., 2015; Dickinson & Porche, 2011; Justice et al., 2018). Extended conversations are particularly important for multilingual learners. Some researchers describe these extended conversations as "more than 'good job!'", where simple praise stops a conversation exchange in its tracks, as illustrated by the stop sign in the chart (Wasik et al., 2022). The next section describes contexts that research shows are ideal for Strive-for-Five conversations. The final section of the chapter offers practical strategies we have seen teachers use to help set the stage for conversations.

When to Engage Kids in Strive-for-Five Conversations

Three routines are especially good for engaging in Strive-for-Five conversations (Cabell, DeCoster, et al., 2013; Gest et al. 2006; Hadley et al., 2022; Weisberg et al., 2016), which are most likely already parts of your day:

1. Interactive Read-Alouds
2. Guided Play
3. Small Groups

Interactive Read-Alouds

It is hard to overstate how important read-alouds are to later reading (National Early Literacy Panel, 2008). Of all the contexts for conversations that researchers have studied, interactive read-aloud is the one they've studied most and the one that consistently benefits student's language comprehension (Dickinson & Porche, 2011; Mol et al., 2009; Pillinger & Vardy, 2022; Whitehurst et al., 1994; Wasik & Hindman, 2011b). During a read-aloud, the teacher reads a book to the whole class or a small group and discusses it with students. A quality book provides multiple opportunities for students to engage in conversation. Students also learn more vocabulary when teachers reread the same book multiple times (Biemiller & Boote, 2006). In Chapter 4 we provide guidance on selecting quality books.

Children's language skills benefit most when teachers have well-organized read-aloud routines (Cabell et al., 2019). Here, we explain ways to manage interactive read-alouds to support Strive-for-Five conversations, and you will find lots more tips for read-alouds throughout this book. For now, think about how to embrace a "conversations count" mindset during read-alouds and how you will organize read-aloud routines. First, think about how you will pace the read-aloud. You'll want to balance keeping students engaged in the text, while engaging them in conversation at key points. Teachers make read-alouds effective when they ask questions during them (Baker et al., 2013; Gonzalez et al. 2014). We recommend these types of conversations:

- **Before reading** Preview an important guiding question to give students a purpose for listening to this book as you read it for the first time or perhaps a repeated reading. You might preview some important vocabulary words in the text.
- **During reading** Choose a few places in the text that will invite conversation, such as pivotal moments in a story or points where an inference or prediction can be made. Pause to elaborate on the important vocabulary words or build knowledge about the book's content.
- **After reading** Ask at least two students to answer the overarching, guiding question you asked before reading. From there, Strive-for-Five conversations can naturally unfold.

Students will also ask questions and make comments during read-alouds which you should acknowledge and allow to inform your own talking points. Pacing read-alouds to include conversations helps students build a mental representation of the text, as well as increase their vocabulary and knowledge.

Think about your designated time for a daily read-aloud and whether there are additional times in the day for it. Teachers usually read books that invite Strive-for-Five conversations during their language arts instruction. If you're teaching in a one-way/transitional bilingual classroom, you should read books that elicit extended conversations in *both* languages, not just the student's dominant language because this ensures multilingual learners are building advanced vocabulary across their languages (Carlo et al., 2004).

Guided Play

Young children learn so much through play (Golinkoff et al., 2006; Quinn et al., 2018). That is why it is important to offer daily opportunities for two kinds: free play and guided play. *Free play* is child-directed; children explore materials and engage in activities entirely on their own. *Guided play* is child-directed, too, but the teacher scaffolds students' language (Hirsh-Pasek et al., 2008). Guided play gives you opportunities to support language as you advance children's play by engaging them in conversation or suggesting more complex ideas for play. To transform free play into guided play, join in. Be curious about what the children are doing. Then strike up a conversation about what you notice. Here are some examples for typical situations:

Pretend Play Center "Wow, you're dressed as a veterinarian! Why are these animals visiting the vet today?"

Art Center "You've used three colors in a pattern. What are your plans for this piece? How do you plan to finish it?"

Outdoor Play "It looks like you're enjoying swinging. If you decide that you want to swing higher, what could you do?"

Note that your role is like a stage manager's. You want children to run the show, but with guidance and support that you gradually release (Stanton-Chapman, 2015). This is particularly important during center time when you give students some choice in how they work or play as they practice skills and repeat activities that you have introduced. In preschool and kindergarten classrooms, set aside time during centers to physically get down to the students' level and have conversations with them. In first-grade classrooms, you may have fewer play-based centers, but you can still integrate playful centers/workstations (e.g., art, writing) and you can look for opportunities to guide play during outdoor time. Conversation during guided play is like a mirror—when you use more complex language, children also use it, and vice versa (Justice et al., 2013).

You can enhance Strive-for-Five conversations by pairing them with novel or interesting activities that spark student-led peer conversations (Hadley et al., 2020). Before students can work collaboratively and talk during centers, you have to teach them how to do the center activities and how to talk about them. A sign of success is when you hear the "hum" of Strive-for-Five conversations amongst peers. Activities that require students to talk about numbers, patterns, or other reasoning skills are excellent for sparking student-led conversations and collaborative learning (Bambha et al., 2022; Gaudreau et al., 2021). To develop literacy skills at centers, adding writing tools encourages students to work together to make lists, signs, or other instructions (Roskos & Christie, 2001). When you purchase items for your classroom centers or outdoor play, consider some that require partner play. When creating partners or groups of children to work at centers together, you may want to pair multilingual learners with native English speakers who can model more advanced language and keep conversations going. You may want to encourage well-matched partners to work together in other center activities so that students can continue practicing skills such as literacy (McMaster et al., 2008; Silverman et al., 2016).

Small-Group Activities

Another great time to engage students in Strive-for-Five conversations is during daily small-group activities. Generally, activities involve two to five students. Under the teacher's guidance, students may practice using new vocabulary, reading and writing complex sentences, and exploring concepts deeply. You can also simplify tasks or review what you've taught in small groups. Conversations allow you to fine-tune instruction to be more responsive and match each learners' needs. One study found that small-group instruction in preschool could be up to 10 times more effective than whole-group instruction, likely due to the scaffolding, which is aligned with students' needs (Connor et al., 2006).

Multilingual learners particularly benefit from small-group language activities. For example, multilingual learners benefit from small groups that focus on discussing texts and vocabulary or drawing and writing in response to texts (Gersten et al., 2007; Proctor et al., 2020; Zucker, Carlo et al., 2021). It's important to provide multilingual learners with routine, targeted small-group instruction because it gives them multiple opportunities to engage in Strive-for-Five conversations and receive your scaffolding. It also provides them with multiple opportunities to say and use focal vocabulary words. You may also want to use small groups to build multilingual learners' background knowledge and provide them with clear

Support Multilingual Learners in Conversations

Strive-for-Five conversations are helpful to multilingual learners, but they may require extra guidance and supports (Goldenberg, 2013; National Academies of Sciences, Engineering, and Medicine, 2017). Here are some suggestions:

- Build on students' home languages and experiences as you introduce new content. If you can translate content into the students' home languages, it may provide a bridge to learning key vocabulary or following instructions.
- Present information using multiple modalities—speech along with gestures, images, objects, physical responses, drawing, and/or writing.
- Gradually present and review content and vocabulary in multiple situations so students have repeated opportunities to interact with them.

Chapter 5 provides more information on how to create multiple modes for learning new vocabulary. Chapter 6 includes nonverbal gestures all learners can use to signal ways they are using advanced verbal reasoning.

explanations of the topics you're studying. Consider how you can use your small-group time with multilingual learners strategically, multiple times per week.

When considering how to form small groups, you may focus on students with similar language needs. For example, these types of homogeneous small groups are part of Multi-tiered System of Support (MTSS) models that many schools use to provide more individualized and intensive instruction to students who need extra support in areas such as vocabulary (Gonzalez et al., 2022; Spencer et al., 2015) or students with limited English proficiency. Alternatively, you may find that you can weave five to seven minutes of language support into your existing, targeted small groups (Solari et al., 2018). Other approaches combine language support activities with small groups that target social-emotional skills (Blewitt et al., 2019).

Practical Tools for Making Conversations Routine

This section explains two tools that effective teachers use to make Strive-for-Five conversations part of their daily classroom routines: equity sticks and turn and talk. As you read about them, notice how both of them include a visual aid to give students a clear reminder of expectations for conversations. Many teachers tell us that these tools are essential because they give children steps to follow as they learn how conversations work. The tools also remind teachers to maintain a conversations count mindset.

Equity Sticks

Equity sticks are a tool you can use for calling on students—simple popsicle sticks with students' names written on them—that signal that it is one child's turn to have a conversation with you. A preschool teacher, Ms. Jackson, told us that this tool is important because before using them, her students  "would get bored or fidgety, and they wouldn't pay attention to me." But after she explained that equity sticks would be how they took turns having conversations during read-alouds and small groups, her students "got used to the routine of taking turns, knowing they would each get a turn sooner or later." She also noticed that all students paid attention to her question because their stick might get chosen to answer the question. Moreover, all students learned to wait instead of calling out answers to questions, which is an important aspect of self-regulation. Here's how Ms. Jackson introduced equity sticks to her students:

Explain the sticks' purpose "In this cup, I have sticks with all of your names on them. Sometimes I will pick a student to answer a question by drawing a name from this cup."

Define equity "This is a fair way to make sure everyone gets a turn to talk. We call these sticks 'equity sticks' because *equity* means being fair and giving everyone a chance to learn."

Link to respect "Good learners show respect for one another. Showing *respect* means being kind and helpful, and following the rules. The rule for equity sticks is to keep the answer in your mind until your stick is chosen. When we use equity sticks, we show respect for one another."

Many teachers use equity sticks as a reminder for themselves that when they "pick a stick," it is time to adopt the conversations count mindset and elicit a Strive-for-Five conversation.

See a teacher use equity sticks to organize Strive-for-Five conversations.

How to Use Equity Sticks

1. Ask a question. Wait 1 or 2 seconds to give thinking time and to discourage students from calling out.

2. Draw an equity stick and name the child. Repeat the question.

3. Ask that student to respond to the question.

4. Follow up with a question that matches that student's response.

   - Scaffold upward to add challenge or downward to simplify the original question.

   - Build trust by sticking to the one student whose stick you drew for a full Strive-for-Five conversation, rather than jumping midway to another student.

5. Allow the student to respond again.

6. Rephrase or extend the student's words.

7. Place used equity sticks upside down to ensure all students with names facing up get a turn for Strive-for-Five conversations at some point that day.

Turn and Talk

To be good conversation partners, students must listen actively to the speaker. To become active listeners, they must receive lots of practice opportunities and support from you. You do that by routinely modeling what active listening looks like. But you can also help students "turn and talk" to learn how to have conversations with their peers. Every few months, you can use the downloadable "Turn and Talk" chart to assign each student a partner who he or she turns toward regularly to discuss a question or topic. Demonstrate how partners look at and listen to each other, use nonverbal cues (eye contact, head nods), and respond in a way that shows they listened. There's value in explicitly teaching these social aspects of using language because young children are still learning not just what to say but how to say it in different situations (Ramsook et al., 2020). *Pragmatic language skills* are the social aspects of using language for conveying formal and informal messages to match the setting.

Keep in mind, your students' family backgrounds may impact their learning style and whether it is more collaborative or independent, as well as the extent to which they use body language and eye contact during conversations (Akechi et al., 2013; Alcalá, et al., 2014). You may never know for sure if a student's background has different norms for conversations, but you can respect differences by not requiring every child to do traditional things such as maintain eye contact. Explain expectations for turn and talk during whole- and small-group instruction and provide support by guiding pairs of students as they practice. When students have mastered turn and talk in pairs, encourage them to talk in less structured settings such as mealtimes or center time. Here is how Ms. Asher asked her kindergartners to practice the pragmatics of good conversations:

Learning Partners

RED	BLUE
Samantha	Chloe
Rhianna	Kiara
Luiz	Luiz
Danny	Fernando

Download a blank copy of the "Learning Partners" chart.

Teacher Reminders "Today we have a new list of learning partners! Your learning partner is someone you'll have conversations with. You'll take turns listening to each other's ideas and questions, and sharing your thoughts."

"Learning Partners" Chart "This chart shows your name and your learning partner's name. Half of your names are on the blue side and half are on the red side. We will take turns so that some days red partners go first and other days blue partners go first. Today red partners go first."

Students Model "Before we turn and talk about today's guiding question, let's have one pair of learning partners show us how to do that. Then you will all have a turn." Ms. Asher asks two students to come up and model and provides specific praise/feedback. "You both did a great job sharing your ideas. I noticed how Jacob nodded to show he was listening, and he responded to learn more by asking another question."

Turn and Talk "I am excited to hear the rest of you share your ideas with your learning partners. When I count you down, you'll 'turn and talk' about the guiding question with your partner. Ready? 1, 2, 3, turn knee-to-knee." Ms. Asher circulates the room and provides support and feedback. "We have about 10 seconds left so please finish up sharing. Now, 1, 2, 3, turn back to me. That was wonderful to hear you all sharing your ideas as you turned and talked. Now you're ready to draw and write about this question in your journals, so let's transition back to our tables."

Watch teachers use turn and talk to support peer conversations.

When you encourage peer conversations in less structured settings such as mealtime and outdoor play, you enhance social skills (Domitrovich et al., 2009). After practicing turn and talk with your students for several weeks in whole-class and small groups, give students other opportunities to talk with each other. We recommend you help peers have conversations with each other with these types of conversation starters:

- **Meal/snack time** "Friends, as we have apples for our snack today, turn to your neighbors and ask them to tell you about the most delicious fruit they have eaten. After you learn their favorite fruit, ask them where it usually comes from."

- **Centers** "As you two friends read at the classroom library, you might stop and share a page you think is interesting in a book. Then ask your friend what he or she notices on that page, too."

- **Outdoor play/recess** "As we walk outside today, turn to your buddy and ask your buddy to tell you something interesting he or she sees in the sky."

Be Sensitive to Children's Cultural Backgrounds

Children may be encouraged to learn and converse differently at home than they do at school because of their cultural backgrounds (Akechi et al., 2013; Alcalá, et al., 2014). Some students may thrive during structured activities with clear solutions, whereas others may thrive when given more open-ended, exploratory activities (Hsu, 2020). Consider offering a variety of interactive activities that complement a variety of learning norms, as some families may emphasize collaborative learning and others may promote more individualized learning (Silva et al., 2015). For example, a student who is looking around may appear to be off-task, but if he or she is used to more collaborative ways of learning, you might view this behavior as cultural and not problematic. Think of ways to give your students collaborative work and independent work.

Another strategy suggested by Hadley and colleagues (2020) is to give students "tokens" or counters that represent conversation turns and guide students to "spend" them by taking conversation turns with a partner. Adding tools such as equity sticks and turn and talk to your daily schedule serves as a reminder for teachers that it is time to embrace a conversations count mindset and elicit a Strive-for-Five conversation.

Final Word: Create Routines for Strive-For-Five Conversations

This chapter considered daily decisions and situations that create space for engaging conversations. Creating routines in your classroom can ensure and support ongoing Strive-for-Five conversations that boost language comprehension and foster student-teacher relationships as well as peer relationships within your classroom. The consistency provided by adding meaningful conversations throughout your daily schedule using tools that become routine for your students can make this addition as seamless as other routines in your space.

Reflect and Implement

- Where in your schedule do most conversations occur and who are they between—teacher-student or student-student?
- How might you use formal language to elevate those conversations?
- In what ways do you ensure that all voices are being heard in your classroom, particularly voices of multilingual learners or students with limited language or social skills?
- What contexts work best for your Strive-for-Five conversations? Discuss interactive read-alouds, guided play, and small-group instructional settings.

FUELING LANGUAGE COMPREHENSION THROUGH CONVERSATIONS

PART II

CHAPTER 4

Choosing Books...

That Spark Rich Conversations

We love reading books to young children! You probably do, too! And, admittedly, we tend to gravitate toward reading narrative genres. There are so many classic stories that are a joy to share with kids, and new ones coming out every day. But young children benefit from exposure to a balance of narrative and informational texts (Duke et al., 2021).

The *literacy knowledge* strand of the Reading Rope refers to knowing how print works, which includes understanding genres, text structures, and text features so students can use texts for various purposes.

When you select texts to support language comprehension, you want to find books with enough advanced content to warrant extended conversations. This chapter explains how diverse genres support conversations. It also provides a checklist for selecting quality texts and reminds you of the text features young children need to be taught during read-alouds.

Building Language Comprehension by Reading Diverse Texts

Whether planning read-alouds or stocking your classroom library, it is important to expose students to a variety of text genres, including narrative and informational. Exposing children to informational texts early on builds knowledge of topics about the natural and social world. Narrative texts entertain and tell stories that often increase children's understanding of social situations when characters solve problems, manage emotions, or learn lessons.

There are many ways to classify text genres and subgenres (Duke & Bennett-Armistead, 2003). When lesson planning to expose children to diverse genres, we find it useful to think of two big categories of text genres:

- *Narrative* texts entertain the reader by sharing an imagined or real experience, usually in story form. This genre is also called fiction.

- *Informational* texts inform the reader by providing facts about the natural or social world. This genre is also called nonfiction.

Terms to Know

Dual-Purpose Genres are texts that include elements of both narrative and informational features and are written to entertain and provide facts.

Informational Genres are a type of text written primarily to provide facts about the natural or social world.

Literacy Knowledge refers to knowing how print works, which includes understanding genres, text structures, and text features so students can use texts for various purposes.

Narrative Genres are a type of text written primarily to entertain or share an experience, usually in story form.

What Is This Book's Genre?

Sometimes it can be tricky to determine whether a book you are considering is a narrative or informational text, especially if you are browsing a library or bookstore website. The chart below may help. It breaks down each major genre into subcategories and lists specific elements to look for (Donovan & Smolkin, 2002; Pentimonti et al., 2011). But there are also many books that blur the lines between genres, called dual-purpose genre texts. *Dual-purpose genres* are texts that include elements of both narrative and informational genres and are written to entertain and provide facts (Bintz & Ciecierski, 2017).

Genre and Subcategories	Key Benefits	Typical Elements
Narrative • Linear narrative that presents characters, setting, problem and solution • Nonlinear narrative that presents events or characters with twists or turns that are not a simple sequence	• Develops students' social skills such as emotional understanding and perspective-taking • Provides models for telling personal narratives, which may include information about setting, key events, and problems and solutions	• "Once upon a time…" • Talking animals • Make-believe or fantasy • Characters portrayed in sequence of events • Illustrations or photos
Informational • Topical research or textbooks that detail a subject • "How to" books that explain procedures • News articles or magazines that explain current events	• Builds knowledge of the world, sparks curiosity, and develops understanding of content-area topics and subtopics • Orients children to important topics and then provides descriptions or key attributions of the events or subject of study	• "The term… means" • Technical vocabulary • Timeless or passive verbs • Academic terms like "predict, observe" • Photos, diagrams, charts, figures
Dual-Purpose • Sequence of events told by a character or narrator that convey an experience alongside accurate information • Historical biography or autobiography	• Presents factual information in an accessible, hybrid format by telling a story • May interweave accurate information and fantasy or imagined elements	• Accurate information • Characters (human, animal, or other) experience realistic events. • Make-believe elements may add excitement.

Students benefit from informational texts by gaining content knowledge and from narrative texts by learning about perspectives, challenges, and the emotional well-being of others. Be sure to expose students to subcategories of narrative and informational genres listed in the first column of the table on the previous page.

For example, a linear narrative such as *The Three Little Pigs* and other classic folktales are organized to include goal-based actions of the main character and includes a setup, initiating event, internal reaction, internal plan, attempts, consequence, and reaction (Duke & Bennett-Armistead, 2003). Some narratives, however, do not follow that typical linear path and may be more circular, such as *If You Give a Mouse a Cookie* by Laura Numeroff. You can help students see how various stories are entertaining or help us learn lessons.

You can also help students to understand when they are reading an informational text that is factual. You can often tell you're reading nonfiction texts when you come across definitions of technical vocabulary or comparisons of perspectives of concepts or historical events. For example, *From Seed to Plant* by Gail Gibbons or *My Five Senses* by Aliki are informational texts for young children.

The third type are dual-purpose texts that present at least some accurate information within a story or using narrative elements. For example, The Magic School Bus series by Joanna Cole tells stories of magical field trips Ms. Frizzle takes with her students while also explaining information about various informational topics. Other books, such as *Growing Vegetable Soup* by Lois Ehlert, do not contain fantasy but convey information about how plants grow from a young narrator's perspective. Historical narratives for young children can present complex topics in a narrative format that allows children to consider past events, such as stories about the civil rights era portrayed by Angela Johnson in *A Sweet Smell of Roses*. Exposing students to a variety of different types of genres helps build a full range of literacy knowledge (Maloch & Bomer, 2013).

Teaching Students Components of Literacy Knowledge

While reading aloud, ask children questions to help build their literacy knowledge of genres, text structures, and text features, which is the fifth strand in the language comprehension section of the Reading Rope. Your expectations for preschoolers should be different from those for K–1 students. For example, preschoolers are likely still developing alphabetic knowledge and an understanding of how print works. In contrast, by the middle of kindergarten, most children have had more experience with texts and, therefore, are ready to think about text organization and text features that support comprehension, such as illustrations, charts, and figures. The chart below provides sample questions to ask children to grow their literacy knowledge (Zucker et al., 2009, 2013).

 Watch a kindergarten teacher discuss some informational text features.

Questions to Grow Literacy Knowledge

Topic	Preschool	Grades K–1
Genre	How can you tell if this story is real or make-believe?	What genre is this—narrative or informational?
	What clues tell you this is a make-believe book?	Why do you think the author wrote the text in this genre?
Text Structures	Which direction do I hold the book and turn the pages?	What headings help organize the information in this book?
	What should I do to keep reading when I get to the end of this page?	How can the figure/diagram/chart help you understand this idea?
Text Features	How does the illustration help you understand the story?	How do the bolded words, italics, or bullet points help you understand this book?
	How does this font or size of text match how the character is feeling?	How can you use the glossary/table of contents/index in this book?

Point Out Key Words for Text Structures

Students benefit when you point out key words that signal common text structures. Genre refers to the entire text, whereas passages within texts often follow predictable structures. There are five common ways authors structure texts that students benefit from understanding because it can enhance comprehension (Meyer & Wijekumar, 2007; Wijekumar et al., 2020). The chart below shows key words you can point out and ask students about when reading aloud.

Text Structure	Key Words	Sample Questions
Comparison	• same, alike, like • different, unlike • special, unique	• Who does… compare to…? • How is this character unlike that character? • What is different/unique about…?
Cause and Effect	• cause, reason, made happen • effect, outcome, impact • because, since	• How did… cause…? • What is the reason that… happened? • What might have been different if…?
Problem and Solution	• problem, puzzle, challenge, trouble • solution, answer, resolution, way out	• What is the problem they are trying to fix? • Why are they having trouble? • How did the characters solve… problem?
Sequence	• first, second, third • beginning, end	• What series of events caused…? • How did things change from the beginning to the end?
Description	• types, kinds, varieties, categories • features, characteristics, traits, qualities	• How did the author describe the character? • When you are learning about (topic), what kinds of… are included? • What are the qualities of…(category)?
Procedural	• "how to…" • step 1, 2, 3 • first, second, third	• What important steps did you notice to do this science activity? • What steps did the characters take to…?

Ramping Up Informational Read-Alouds

Exposure to informational texts in early grades prepares children to understand texts they will learn from in later grades. There is ample evidence that early childhood teachers tend to read aloud mostly narrative texts even though informational texts are important for building students' vocabulary and knowledge (Duke & Carlisle, 2011; Pentimonti et al., 2011). There are likely various reasons for the limited number of informational text read-alouds. Here are two common misconceptions about informational text read-alouds that may explain why many teachers are less inclined to read informational texts:

- **Misconception:** The genre doesn't matter as long as the kids are engaged during read-alouds.
  - **Fact:** Listening to narrative texts and informational texts involves different regions of the brain (Jacoby & Fedorenko, 2020). We want to build our students' neural pathways for understanding *both* genres of texts.
- **Misconception:** Informational texts on science and social studies topics are boring.
  - **Fact:** Kids don't always find informational texts boring because they love learning about the world around them. In fact, many young children prefer informational texts (Kotaman & Tekin, 2017; Correia, 2011).

We challenge you to integrate more informational texts into your read-alouds. There's not a precise formula for how often you should read informational texts to students. Some experts recommend balancing exposure to narrative and informational texts to ensure students are ready for college and careers that demand strategic research (Pappas, 2006).

As you read aloud more informational texts, you are likely to find that your students not only enjoy them, but gain noteworthy knowledge from them (Neuman & Kaefer, 2018a and 2018b; Pollard-Durodola et al., 2022). For adults and children, it is often more difficult to comprehend informational texts than narrative texts (Clinton et al., 2020). Strive-for-Five conversations about informational texts builds students' knowledge of the genre and ability to comprehend those texts. You might want to introduce young children to a topic of study with a read-aloud of a narrative text or dual-purpose text, and then an informational text. It may be easier to build topic-related vocabulary and content knowledge with a narrative text or dual-purpose text before asking young children to learn from an informational text (Bintz & Ciecierski, 2017; Neuman & Kaefer, 2018a and 2018b; Zucker et al., 2019). See Chapter 7 for more on selecting text sets that systematically build knowledge.

Infuse Your Classroom With Informational Texts

PreK, kindergarten, and first-grade students have access to fewer informational texts than narrative texts in the classroom and home (MacKay et al., 2020; Yopp & Yopp, 2006). Unless you bring informational texts into your classroom, your students may have exposure to them only one to two minutes per day (Duke & Carlisle, 2011).

Furthermore, our research shows many early childhood teachers tend to read aloud narrative genres (Pentimonti et al., 2010, 2011). We asked PreK teachers to keep a list of the read-aloud titles they chose during a 30-week period (Pentimonti et al., 2011). We looked up over 11,000 titles teachers read during a school year and coded them: narrative, informational, or dual-purpose. The pie chart at right shows what teachers reported reading. Only 17% were informational in nature, including the traditional nonfiction genre and mixed or dual-purpose genre.

Informational genres in this study conveyed accurate information about the natural or social world in a non-narrative format. Dual-purpose genres had a dual purpose of telling a story while conveying accurate information. This equates to about one minute per school day spent on informational read-alouds. We encourage you to integrate more informational books into your collection, and we have worked to develop curricula that provide half narratives and half informational genres (Zucker et al., 2019). However, good news may be emerging from more recent research that shows closer to that balance in some schools (Wang et al., 2023).

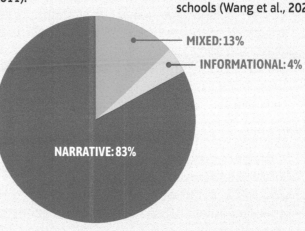

MIXED: 13%

INFORMATIONAL: 4%

NARRATIVE: 83%

Choosing Quality Read-Aloud Texts

Children's level of interest in and enjoyment of an interactive read-aloud depends largely on the texts you choose. To select texts that facilitate Strive-for-Five conversations, you want a text that is not only interesting but also contains multiple vocabulary words worth learning and topics that stimulate conversation. Below are three key features of texts that support Strive-for-Five conversations:

1. The Text Contains Rich Vocabulary.

Choose a text with rich vocabulary that your students need to learn. Quality children's books contain 50% more vocabulary than spoken language, when compared to college graduates' discourse (Cunningham & Stanovich, 1991). In fact, when children are read to routinely in the first five years of life, they are exposed to 1.4 million more words than children who are not (Logan et al., 2019). In Chapter 5, we explain words that warrant direct instruction and how to teach them to children. For now, simply read through any read-aloud book you're considering to confirm that it has multiple words your students would benefit from knowing—perhaps five or six unfamiliar words. But do not worry if a great book contains fewer. In Chapter 5, we explain how to "import" topic-related words.

2. The Text Requires Abstract Thinking.

To develop strong language comprehension, select texts that require some advanced or abstract thinking, such as inferring, problem-solving, and reasoning about cause-effect relationships. (See Chapter 6 for more on abstract reasoning.) During read-aloud, teachers tend to push children to use these higher-level reasoning skills only when they come to pages that contain higher-level topics (Zucker et al., 2010). This makes sense. After all, Strive-for-Five conversations usually start with something from a book that sparks discussion. So select stories that will require students to grapple with the characters' complex emotions or problems that they are trying to solve. Select informational texts that present facts and ideas that will spark readers' curiosity about how things work and inferring conditions that could change things. Also, check informational and dual-purpose genre texts for accuracy and talk to students about what is inaccurate (Donovan & Smolkin, 2001). Some children's books, such as the classic *The Very Hungry Caterpillar* by Eric Carle, can perpetuate common misconceptions that butterflies make cocoons; however, this book may still be worth reading if you explain that moths make cocoons whereas most butterflies make chrysalises and ask students why the author may have chosen to say it that way.

3. The Text Addresses High-Priority Instructional Topics.

To set the stage for Strive-for-Five conversations, be sure the book addresses a high-priority instructional topic. That means it might be linked to a unit of study in science or social studies, as detailed in Chapter 7 on knowledge building. Or it might be linked to a social-emotional topic that is important for young children to discuss. Read-alouds are an excellent space to have conversations about vocabulary related to thoughts and feelings or moral decisions characters make (Al Otaiba, 2004). When students learn various emotion words during interactive read-alouds, they are better able to understand and use these words to describe their own feelings (Bierman et al., 2008; Poventud et al., 2015). Again, our research with narratives found that only pages that contain emotion vocabulary inspire Strive-for-Five conversations about high-priority topics (Alvarenga et al., 2020).

Another high-priority topic is representation of multicultural, diverse characters that can help children see themselves in books and increase their curiosity about the world and others' perspectives (Acevedo, 2019; Worthy et al., 2013). Children and parents increasingly want to read books that help them understand new places and worlds, and other people's lives. For example, in one survey of reading preferences, a father said he wants his daughter to learn from books "that people come in all shapes, sizes, colors, beliefs systems, and educational or cultural backgrounds, so that she is ready to engage with the world in an authentic way" (Scholastic, 2019).

Find Great Books

The books you choose to read aloud should capture your core curriculum's topics of study and support Strive-for-Five conversations. Below are some sources. Annual award lists, as well as "best of" lists from bookstores, libraries, and publishers, are all helpful.

- The Caldecott Medal is awarded to the artist/illustrator of a children's picture book.
- The Robert F. Sibert Informational Book Medal is awarded for the best informational book.
- The Coretta Scott King Book Award honors outstanding African American authors and illustrators of children's books.
- The Pura Belpré Awards honors outstanding portrayals of the Hispanic and Latino cultural experience in children's books.
- Reading Rockets has a themed booklist and book finder.
- Scholastic is read-aloud central! Go to the online Teacher Store and search "Read-Aloud Collection" for many great options.

Text Features That Support Strive-for-Five Conversations

Preview a text and answer each question below. If you checked several high-quality features, this text supports meaningful conversations.	Quality		
	High	**Moderate**	**Low**
Can you find at least **five vocabulary words** in the text worth teaching your students?	☐ Yes 5+ words	☐ Maybe 2–4 words	☐ No
If **narrative**, does the text have a **coherent structure,** such as a clear problem and solution?	☐ Yes coherent, accurate	☐ Maybe, with support	☐ No
If **informational**, does the text have **accurate facts** presented in a way young child can understand?			
Does the text address a **content-area topic** (e.g., science, social studies) or **social-emotional topic** (e.g., caring and empathy for others, understanding of others, sharing with others, developing self-confidence)?	☐ Yes	☐ Somewhat	☐ No
Does the text contain **multicultural** characters and topics, languages other than English, or stories about justice and equity?	☐ Yes	☐ Somewhat	☐ No

Download a copy of the checklist.

The chart above can help you select books that lend themselves to Strive-for-Five conversations. Some books do not lend themselves to these extended conversations, such as alphabet books and counting books. For example, asking higher-level thinking questions about a rhythmic alphabet book such as *Chicka Chicka Boom Boom* by Bill Martin, Jr. and John Archambault would not align with the text's focus on the names of letters. Other counting books such as *Five Little Monkeys Jumping on the Bed* lend themselves to talk about numeracy and may be harder to elicit extended conversations. Concept books such as those are still worth reading at other times of the day because they can promote foundational literacy or math skills (Zucker et al., 2009).

In contrast, several researchers have used complex narratives, such as Frank Asch's *Happy Birthday, Moon* and other books in his Bear series, to promote higher-level reasoning skills and, therefore, Strive-for-Five conversations (Price, 2012; van Kleeck et al., 2006). Likewise, well-illustrated informational books by authors such as Gail Gibbons and books with amazing photos such as *National Geographic*'s also invite Strive-for-Five conversations. But consider reading only portions of those books at a time if they contain too much information to hold your students' attention. Additionally, books by authors such as Angela Johnson present multicultural characters and complex historical topics, as well as thought-provoking illustrations, to help you extend conversations.

Final Word: Find Quality Narrative, Informational, and Dual-Purpose Texts

To ensure that your students gain literacy knowledge, read aloud texts in a variety of genres. Work with your colleagues to identify high-quality books or check out lists of award winners and expert recommendations. Remember, you are selecting these titles to promote Strive-for-Five conversations. So, be sure they have enough content worth discussing. Lastly, ask questions that help students think about text genres and text features to prepare them to navigate textbooks and research materials in later grades.

Reflect and Implement

- Think about the books available in your room or the books you have read aloud in the last week. Is there an even mix of narrative and informational text genres? Do you include texts that serve a dual purpose?
- What are some ways that informational texts are useful to your students' learning? How do you use informational texts in your teaching?
- What are some texts that you have read to your students that have required them to use abstract thinking?
- Review the chart on page 65. Can you commit to asking your students one new type of question related to text genre, text use or structure, or text features? How might that question open the door to a Strive-for-Five conversation?

CHAPTER 5

Go Nuts With Words!

Building Vocabulary With Conversations

Vocabulary is one of the strongest predictors of later reading achievement (National Institute of Child Health and Human Development, 2010). So if we want children to become successful readers, we must start building their vocabulary skills early. Let's consider how Strive-for-Five conversations can do that. This one took place between first-grade teacher, Ms. Carr, and her students, on the playground during recess.

1 **MS. CARR:** Wow! Look at you all jumping rope. Are you trying to get *fit*?

2 **ANTHONY:** Yeah.

3 **MS. CARR:** Yes, you're going to be fit and strong with all that exercise.

4 **ANTHONY:** My rope is too small.

5 **MS. CARR:** I see what you mean. It doesn't *fit* the size of your body. You know, *fit* is one of our multiple-meaning words. It can mean whether something is a comfortable size, but it can also mean getting healthy by eating right and exercising. Now, let's see if we can find you a longer jump rope that fits your size so you can get fit and strong!

Ms. Carr is referring to words she's already taught her students, using the vocabulary cards below. She exposes her students to these kinds of multiple-meaning words during read-alouds and at other times of day. Notice she uses relatable synonyms and examples so students understand words more deeply. Young children enjoy learning multiple meanings of the same word. They also enjoy using those words playfully in conversations and in jokes and puns. Consider using the poster to draw students' attention to multiple-meaning words.

Watch this teacher talk about multiple-meaning words.

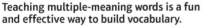

Download the poster.

Teaching multiple-meaning words is a fun and effective way to build vocabulary.

Good Readers Know LOTS of Words

The vocabulary strand of Scarborough's Reading Rope makes it clear that children need breadth and depth of word knowledge to comprehend texts. So we must focus on *both* in our teaching.

Breadth To comprehend texts and conversations, children need to know *lots* of words. When you expose them to the meaning of lots of advanced words, they build a wide breadth of vocabulary.

Depth To use advanced words in speaking and writing, children need deep knowledge of what words mean and how to use them in sentences. You can deepen children's knowledge of words using Strive-for-Five conversations that include focal vocabulary.

When we repeatedly hear and use a new word, we move from a shallow understanding of that word to a deeper, higher-quality understanding of it and of how to use it, pronounce it, and eventually spell it (Perfetti, 2007). This progression might start with understanding a new word when someone says it to using it in speaking or writing. When we understand a word accurately,

Terms to Know

Cognates are words that share a similar root word across languages and have a similar pronunciation and the same meaning (e.g., *vocabulary* in English and *vocabulario* in Spanish). They are easier to remember if we know the word in our first language.

Expressive Vocabulary are words we use to convey meaning when we speak or write.

False Cognates are words that sound the same but do not share a meaning across languages.

Morphemes are the smallest units of language that carry meaning. They can be root words (e.g., *girl*, *view*) or smaller units that we combine with root words, such as endings (e.g., *girls*) or affixes (e.g., *review*).

Multiple-Meaning Words are words that are pronounced the same way, but have more

than one definition, such as *spring* (the nouns: season and water source) and *spring* (the verb: to jump up). We also include words that are spelled differently (e.g., *reed*—noun/plant and *read*—verb/literacy act) because young learners need to understand that words that sound the same often have different meanings.

Receptive Vocabulary are words we understand as we read or listen to spoken language.

Semantics is the meaning of words or phrases in a language.

Vocabulary is all the words we know and use. It is also referred to as our *lexicon*.

Word Consciousness is awareness of and excitement for learning new words.

it is part of our *receptive vocabulary* or listening vocabulary. When we can also use that word accurately, it is part of our *expressive vocabulary* or spoken vocabulary. For example, you may be able to understand the phrase "good dog" in a language other than English (Spanish, "Buen perro" or German, "Braver hund"), but only have the spoken fluency to name *dog* and can't yet describe the dog as *good*. Similarly, young children may be able to only understand the word initially, but with more exposure to it, they will likely start to say it or use it accurately when they speak.

You can help students move from shallow to deeper word knowledge by exposing them to new vocabulary on a regular basis. Keep in mind that when children enter school, they need to know 3,000–4,000 words and continue adding thousands of words to their vocabulary each year to become fluent readers (Biemiller, 2010). Of course, typical word learning begins slowly with babies saying first words such as *hi*, *bye*, *mama*, and *dada* around their first birthday (Henrichs et al., 2011). Toddlers' vocabulary seemingly explodes as they move from putting together two-word utterances, such as "More milk," to much longer ones by age three. By the time they reach preschool, most children will know several thousand root words, which can propel them like a "springboard" into adding many more words to their vocabulary (Hadley & Mendez, 2021). Keep in mind that multilingual learners may know words in their first language that they can understand receptively in English, but may still be building knowledge about how to use the word expressively (Mancilla-Martinez et al., 2020).

Depth of Word Knowledge

I understand that word.

Receptive Vocabulary

SHALLOW WORD KNOWLEDGE

- Understanding of the word may be limited to **one or two contexts**.
- Understanding does **not include all aspects** of the word's meaning.
- **Weaker links to spelling and sound**/phonology of the word
- Incomplete **grammatical** understandings linked to the word's use

I use that word correctly.

Expressive Vocabulary

DEEP WORD KNOWLEDGE

- Understanding of the word applies across **multiple contexts.**
- Understanding **includes most aspects** of the word's meaning.
- Knowledge of **similar words** with ability to discriminate meanings
- Stronger **links to spelling and sound**/phonology of the word
- Ability to use the word in a sentence with **correct grammar**

How Children Learn Words

Children can learn words incidentally through exposure to good books or meaningful conversations (Sénéchal, 1997). But they learn words more effectively through direct, explicit instruction (Biemiller & Boote, 2006; Dickinson et al., 2019). You can combine opportunities for incidental word learning with direct vocabulary instruction as outlined below. Moreover, to ensure equitable instruction for multilingual learners and students who enter school with limited vocabularies, provide direct, explicit vocabulary instruction in all content areas (Gersten et al., 2007). Consider how to provide multilingual learners and students who score below benchmark on your school's language screening measures, rich, evidence-based instruction, such as additional small-group instruction to review new vocabulary that was introduced in whole-group instruction (Coyne et al., 2022; Pullen et al., 2010; Zucker et al., 2013). Some schools deliver that instruction as part of a Multi-Tiered System of Support (MTSS), where key vocabulary words are introduced to all students in whole-group or Tier 1 instruction, and are reinforced in small-group or Tier 2 instruction with extra opportunities for practice.

Two Methods for Word Learning

INCIDENTAL WORD LEARNING	DIRECT VOCABULARY INSTRUCTION
• Strive-for-Five conversations	• Pre-teach words in books
• Share book reading	• Teach words in science, history, etc.
• Content-area instruction	• Explain words children ask about

Which Words to Teach

We don't have the time to teach children every word they need to learn. Thus, it is important to consider which words are worth teaching. Researchers have suggested many approaches to help us with this (Beck et al., 2013; Biemiller, 2010). Basic words do not often warrant direct instruction because most students already know them or will learn them easily. Instead, words worth teaching are advanced vocabulary that are important to understanding academic texts (Barnes et al., 2021). It is also worth teaching content-specific words to ensure all kids build knowledge needed for success in school. The chart on the next page summarizes these word categories.

Word Categories	
Basic Words	Common words that **rarely require direct instruction** because children learn them from exposure through conversations and book reading Examples: *baby, car, jump, sad* Word types: concrete nouns and verbs, simple emotions, basic modifiers
Advanced Words	**Domain-general words** that have **precise or complex meanings;** words that warrant explanation or direct instruction because they are key to comprehending texts Examples: *disappoint, competition, advice* Word types: abstract nouns and verbs, complex emotions, nuanced modifiers
Content-Specific Words	**Domain-specific words** that have a precise or **technical meaning** linked to science, engineering, math, music, art, history, or other domain Examples: *recycle, stem/bud/roots, Native American, habitat* Word types: technical nouns and verbs, precise academic concepts

You can likely judge the types of words your students need to be taught (Neuman et al., 2021). Pre-teach a few key words before a science lesson or a read-aloud, keeping in mind that there is a limit to how many to teach in a single session before kids tune out. Here's a guide that's worked for us:

- **Preschool:** pre-teach 2 words
- **Kindergarten:** pre-teach 2–3 words
- **First Grade:** pre-teach 3–4 words

As children move up the grades, the instruction they receive should focus more on sophisticated vocabulary and technical words, and less on basic words. *During* and *after* the lesson or activity, emphasize your chosen words and encourage children to say them and use them in responses. The words you decide are worth time teaching with direct instruction are often called *focal words* in the science of reading research. Give those words a special name to signal to students their importance, such as calling them "wondrous words" or "amazing words."

As we explained in Chapter 4, you can have robust Strive-for-Five conversations about vocabulary if you select quality texts that contain advanced and content-specific words. When reading an informational text, you will likely teach more content-specific words than advanced words. But when reading a narrative, it is fine to teach mostly advanced words because the text will likely not contain many relevant content-specific words. For example, when reading a narrative called *The Pout-Pout Fish* by Deborah Diesen, a kindergarten teacher might consider teaching these advanced words:

1. impolite
2. dreary
3. pout
4. grin
5. hope (vs. hopeless)
6. destined
7. agree
8. advice
9. tentacles

Which of those words would you teach? They are all good candidates. In this case, the teacher had time to teach only six words (three words in each of two read-aloud sessions) so she selected the ones that were most important to comprehending the text, and marked them with asterisks. Next, she decided "encouragement" was an important theme of this book, so she added it to the list. She did not teach basic words, such as *fish*,

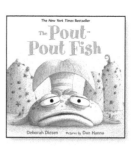

and, instead, simply pointed to the characters/creatures (clam, jellyfish, squid, octopus). She also did not teach the content-specific word *tentacles* because it wasn't explained in the narrative.

1. impolite
2. dreary*
3. pout*
4. grin
5. hope (vs. hopeless)*
6. destined*
7. agree
8. advice*
   encouragement**
9. ~~tentacles~~

Consider selecting words that meet these criteria:

- important to comprehend the book
- advanced or content-specific words
- highly useful words students will encounter again and again in formal language

If you want to read aloud a book over multiple days but it only has a handful of words worth teaching, consider "importing" or bringing in some relevant, advanced words that relate to the book's topic (Beck et al., 2013). For example, a kindergarten teacher read aloud *Owen* by Kevin Henkes because it addresses relevant messages about the challenges of starting school. However, when she went through all the pages she could only find four words worth teaching: *wonderful*, *ratty*, *essential*, and *perfect*. So she "imported" two advanced words that relate to the themes in the book: *mature* and *comfort*.

Check Your Core Curricula for Advanced and Content-Specific Words

In a review of popular reading and writing curricula, researchers discovered little direct instruction of advanced vocabulary words (Wright & Neuman, 2013). 60 to 70% of words taught were basic words rather than advanced and content-specific words.

Review the vocabulary taught in your curricula to determine if the words taught are sophisticated enough and if the methods include explicit instruction. If you teach multilingual learners, most teachers have to modify their core curricula to meet the needs of English learners (EdReports, 2022). That is, you may have to provide more explicit vocabulary instruction and vocabulary picture cards or other visual aids. Also consider if your curricula teaches a range of parts of speech, as most curricula focus on teaching concrete nouns and too few advanced verbs and modifiers (Hadley & Mendez, 2021). Don't be afraid to modify your curriculum, as necessary, to ensure your students learn a variety of important words.

Using Picture Vocabulary Cards

Picture vocabulary cards are the most efficient tool for teaching new words directly and, therefore, should be part of an effective instructional routine (Zucker et al., 2013, 2019, 2021). Here is a sample:

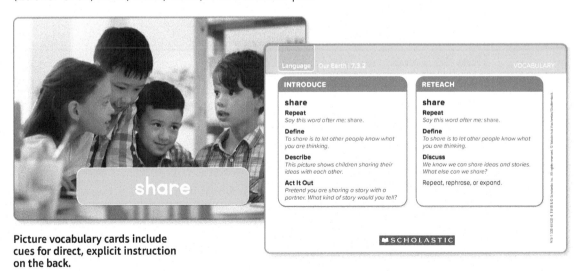

Picture vocabulary cards include cues for direct, explicit instruction on the back.

Some features to notice:

1. They are accessible to children who are learning to decode the word, as well as those who are not quite there yet and are relying on the picture to understand the word.

2. They contain a child-friendly definition of the word. A typical dictionary definition is unhelpful and potentially confusing because of the sophisticated word it likely contains. So use an English learner's dictionary (e.g., *Oxford Learner's Dictionary* online) or a children's dictionary (e.g., *Scholastic Children's Dictionary*, 2019) to prepare a simple definition.

3. They invite children to act out the word, giving them a meaningful opportunity to say and use the word, which is important because many children need a half dozen or more opportunities to use a word before it becomes part of their own vocabulary (Gray & Brinkley, 2011; Kiernan & Gray, 1998).

4. They feature tips on the back, such as talking points for teachers that begin with whole-class approaches and provide reteaching opportunities for students in small groups.

If your curriculum contains these cards, great! If it doesn't, not to worry. You can easily create them. If you don't have time to create cards, consider accessing publicly available collections such as this one we created: https://public.cliengage.org/tools/quality/family-engagement-resources/teaching-together-building-your-childs-vocabulary-workshop.

How to Teach Words Using the Cards

Once you've accessed or created your cards, here's how to use them:

1. **Say the word.** Ask students to repeat the word so that they establish a clear phonological representation of the word in their minds and know how to pronounce it.

2. **Define and explain the word.** Give students the child-friendly definition and explain its link to the picture. Make this part snappy so you don't lose students' attention. We also recommend directly teaching the word's meaning rather than asking young children to guess it, as this often confuses the whole class.

See teachers explicitly teaching new vocabulary.

3. **Act out the word or use it in a sentence.** Invite children to act out the word with you, using gestures or facial expressions. If you can't think of a way to act it out, encourage students to use the word in a meaningful sentence that connects with the picture you're showing.

4. **Revisit and reteach the word.** Plan opportunities to review the word. For example, reference the vocabulary card when you come to the word in a book or use the word in a content-area lesson. For students who need more practice, review words in a small-group session and ask them questions that will give them practice saying and using them.

See how the teacher revisits and reteaches a new vocabulary word.

Improving Outcomes for Multilingual Learners With Direct Vocabulary Instruction

Most multilingual learners will catch up to native English speakers on decoding, but language comprehension is where multilingual learners need the most intentional support to become successful readers (Carlo & Bengochea, 2007; National Assessment of Education Progress, 2022). Routinely providing direct vocabulary instruction ensures equitable access to words for *all* students. For multilingual learners, you can add interactive visual aids (such as picture vocabulary cards) and physical gestures alongside explicit vocabulary definitions (Carlo et al., 2004; Silverman & Hines, 2009; Vadasy et al., 2015). Although some recommend directly teaching more basic words to multilingual learners, teach advanced and content-specific vocabulary, too, as multilingual learners can learn those words with direct instruction (Zucker et al., 2021).

One strategy for multilingual learners is to connect the English word or concept to a word or concept in their native language. For example, *cognate* instruction involves teaching two words: an English word and a word in another language that have similar spellings, pronunciations, and meanings. Even young children have an advantage when learning cognates compared to words that are non-cognates (Pérez et al., 2010; Squires et al., 2020). You can point out cognates to students to improve their word learning by noting when a word in English sounds the same and means the same thing as a word in Spanish or another language your students use at home (Carlo et al., 2004; Pollard-Durodola & Simmons, 2009; Pollard-Durodola et al., 2016; Zucker

If you're multilingual, consider using the downloadable poster to draw students' attention to cognates.

Download the poster.

et al., 2019). You may want to compare cognates across two languages, using vocabulary cards and a quick hand signal. For example, a preschool teacher, Ms. Lester, teaches cognates this way:

1. Early in the school year, she teaches her students what a cognate is and a hand signal they should use when they learn a new word that is a cognate. "When a word in English and a word in Spanish sound alike and have the same meaning, they are called *cognates*."

2. Throughout the year, she notes vocabulary words that are English/Spanish cognates. At the same time, she and her students use the hand signal and may reference the "Cognate" poster. "The word *repeat* in English and *repetir* in Spanish are cognates. They sound alike in both languages and both words mean you will say something again."

3. She also talks to her students about some *false cognates*, which are words that sound the same but do not share a meaning across languages. For example, "We laughed when I thought that the words *embarrassed* in English and *embarazada* in Spanish, were cognates. I said 'Estoy embarazada' thinking it meant 'I am embarrassed,' but this word means *pregnant*."

Another strategy is "bridging" English and the child's home language, using intentional vocabulary translations, that provide an equivalent word for the focal vocabulary words you are directly teaching. You may also intentionally translate certain classroom instructions or information to emphasize important vocabulary. Although technologies are transforming the way we support multilingual learners' vocabulary knowledge (Smith et al., 2023), available technologies are somewhat ahead of rigorous research evidence for the diverse populations of multilingual learners. We recommend using your judgment and knowledge of each English learner's needs to provide support for word learning.

Nurturing Word Consciousness: When Students "Go Nuts" for Words!

As you teach more words, your students will become increasingly *word conscious*. Word consciousness is when you're interested in learning and using new or more precise words. When young children become proud of knowing lots of "big" or advanced words, they develop a positive mindset about long-term learning (Zucker et al., 2021). You can get your students excited about words by playing a game where students put their thumbs up when they hear a word and by having visual reminders of focal words. For example, see the photo of a "We're Nuts for Words!" tree that a preschool teacher developed to signal the importance of those words. You can also consider a way to track and celebrate when students use new vocabulary.

See how students signal with thumbs up the words their teacher pre-taught.

Here are some other approaches from teachers we've worked with:

- **Use a catchy name for focal vocabulary words.** You might call them "wondrous words" and kids who use them "word wizards" to highlight that these words warrant attention.

- **Encourage students to ask about words they hear.** The question "What does _____ mean?" is music to the ears of a teacher who's promoting word consciousness. If your students are old enough to use an online learners' dictionary, they can help you look up the words.

Ms. Esquivel's "wondrous words" of the week

Ms. Henderson's filled-in tracker for her students' use of "wondrous words"

Celebrate when students try using new words. You might fill a "nuts for words" jar with acorns each time students use a focal word. Or you can have students fill in a chart or other system that tallies the use of words. When you've reached a collective word learning goal, have a class celebration, such as bringing a stuffed animal to school, having kids wear crazy socks, or a popcorn party.

Download a blank copy of the word tracker.

Develop Your Own Word Consciousness

Our students don't have to be the only ones learning new words. We can, too! One of the best ways to get excited about the power of words is by learning them together. Some newspapers have a "word of the day" section. That's how I learned the word *petrichor*, a smell I've known since childhood, growing up in hot Texas summers:

Petrichor A pleasant smell that comes with the first rain after a long period of warm, dry weather

Another word I learned recently describes a feeling that I had experienced when our family's major sports opponent lost a big game. It's actually a German word that we do not have an equivalent for in English:

Schadenfreude Rejoicing in, or getting pleasure from the misfortune of others

Language is always evolving. People create new words or use old words in new ways. For example, my daughter recently taught me that the word *slay* has an innovative meaning.

Traditional meaning—**Slay**—to kill a person or animal

New meaning—**Slay**—to do something spectacularly well

I remember my daughter said, "Hollis really slayed the three-pointers in today's game!" I asked her if she meant to say that word and she explained yes, it was a compliment. We looked it up, and sure enough, there's a new meaning for *slay*. Several teachers have told us that once their students "go nuts for words," they do, too.

Promote puns or jokes that play with word meanings. Many jokes contain puns, which can generate excitement for words. For example, if your students recently learned the word *hilarious*, ask, "Did you hear the joke about the little mountain? It's hill-arious!" Maybe spell it out on a dry-erase board to show students how the word play works.

Adults who promote word consciousness in their students often take interest in learning words themselves. Consider how, as an adult, you might find joy in learning new words or alternate word meanings.

Final Word: Build Vocabulary With Strive-for-Five Conversations

It is clear that the vocabulary strand of the Reading Rope is essential for your students to become successful readers. The ideas in this chapter build on the Strive-for-Five framework because new vocabulary words are presented in the context of a meaningful conversation. Celebrate when students spontaneously use new words with praise as well as questions that keep vocabulary-focused conversation going. Or when you hear a student talking about a concept related to a recently taught vocabulary word, consider whether you can stretch that conversation for a few more turns to get the student to say and use a "wondrous word." Finally, challenge yourself to weave vocabulary words you're learning into classroom transitions, outdoor play, or mealtime. These sorts of Strive-for-Five opportunities are highly effective when they include important words you want students to learn to become successful readers.

> ### *Reflect and Implement*
>
> How do you carry out vocabulary instruction with your students?
>
> How do you select words to teach?
>
> In what ways do your curricular materials support explicit vocabulary instruction? Do you need to refresh those materials to meet your learners' needs?

CHAPTER 6

Show What You Know...

Supporting Verbal Reasoning With Conversations

With her preschool students, Ms. Palmer is reading aloud *Do Like Kyla* by Angela Johnson. She knows that her students need to integrate their existing background knowledge with information in the text to have a deeper understanding. Ms. Palmer plays an important role in guiding children to practice this through Strive-for-Five conversations that require *verbal reasoning* to explain ideas aloud or think about and learn new information. Consider her classroom read-aloud conversation on the next page and how it moves from a simple, concrete understanding of the text to a more complex, abstract understanding of it.

Ms. Palmer's open-ended questions about the book move children from concrete to abstract understanding. Open-ended questions that begin with *wh-* words and *how* usually elicit more than a one-word answer (Deshmukh et al., 2019). (See the discussion of open-ended questions on page 19 in Chapter 1.) Be sure to ask a combination of concrete and abstract questions during every read-aloud, as Ms. Palmer does in the Strive-for-Five conversation below.

- **Concrete questions** are literal. Readers can answer them using details in the text. The author's words or the illustrations give children the information they need to answer the questions.

- **Abstract questions** require complex thinking or for children to assemble information from the text with their background knowledge. These tend to be open-ended question

Conversation About *Do Like Kyla*

1. **Concrete** teacher question: What is the weather like?
2. Student: Snowy and sunny.
3. **Abstract** teacher question: Yes, it was snowy, but the sun was shining. Why do you think the snow makes a *crunch* sound?
4. Student: Because they are walking in it.
5. Teacher **extends**: Yes, I bet the snow was deep enough to make a *crunch* sound when they stepped on it, but the sun wasn't strong enough to melt the snow and make a *slush*, *slush* sound.

Mama says, "Lots of sunshine today."

Got me some purple snow boots like Kyla, and we both crunch, crunch in the snow all the way to the store.

How do you know the first question is concrete? The author told you that there was lots of sunshine and that there was snow. Information about the weather is provided on multiple pages. Why is the second question abstract? It pushes you to go beyond what the author says and integrate what students might know about how snow feels and sounds using information from the text.

Mr. Diaz is reading *Ramona the Pest* by Beverly Cleary to his first graders and having several Strive-for-Five conversations. Like Ms. Palmer, Mr. Diaz asks concrete and abstract questions, but he asks more of the latter because his students are older. He stops after reading the third paragraph about Ramona and her neighbor, Howie, preparing to go trick-or-treating:

> Howie walked stolidly along, lugging his tail, so Ramona ran out to meet him. He was not wearing a mask, but instead had pipe cleaners Scotch-taped to his face for whiskers.
>
> "I'm the baddest witch in the world," Ramona informed him, "and you can be my cat."
>
> "I don't want to be your cat," said Howie. "I don't want to be a cat at all."

Terms to Know

Abstract Questions require children to put information together from parts of the text read aloud or to use background knowledge to answer correctly.

Abstract Thinking is higher-level thinking about things beyond the tangible to consider connections, patterns, relationships, and solve complex problems.

Causal Reasoning is higher-level thinking about how things affect one another.

Concrete Questions are literal questions that are answered with information from the text.

Concrete Thinking is basic thinking about things that you can see, hear, touch, or use to describe something tangible or illustrated in the text.

Guiding Questions are questions that address an overarching idea in a read-aloud text. They are previewed before reading and answered after reading with a series of Strive-for-Five conversations.

Inference Making is a type of abstract thinking that is important to understanding texts because it uses evidence in the text with reasoning to draw a conclusion.

Instructional Units are a series of lessons that address a broad topic or theme and address multiple curriculum areas, such as language arts combined with science, math, or social studies.

Verbal Reasoning is using language to explain ideas or think about and learn new information.

Mr. Diaz then asked these open-ended questions about the passage that followed.

Howie walked stolidly along, lugging his tail, so Ramona ran out to meet him. He was not wearing a mask, but instead had pipe cleaners Scotch-taped to his face for whiskers.	**Concrete:** What was on Howie's face? *Possible answer:* His whiskers are held on with tape.
	Abstract: What can you infer about his costume if he had to use tape to attach the whiskers to his face? *Possible answer:* His costume was made at home or in a rush. The tape on his face probably feels sticky. **Abstract:** Why do you think the author mentioned this detail that Howie is "lugging" his cat tail? Lugging means you carry something with great effort. *Possible answer:* He didn't like his costume. You could see that he was frustrated that he had to carry that heavy tail around.

Asking Abstract Questions

Our research in early childhood classrooms shows that 86% of questions teachers ask during read-alouds are concrete and easy for children to answer (Deshmukh et al., 2019). It is fine to ask such questions to check comprehension or as a downward scaffold, but you should also ask more challenging, *abstract questions* that begin with *Why...* and *What if....* When you ask abstract questions, your students need to use abstract thinking to answer them.

Abstract thinking is higher-level thinking about connections, patterns, relationships, and complex problems and solutions. It relates to the verbal reasoning strand of Scarborough's Reading Rope, which focuses on children's abilities to make inferences and reason about complex language in books.

For read-alouds, plan questions that fall along the continuum below, which moves from the most basic, concrete ideas to more abstract ideas that require making inferences and backing up claims with evidence from the text (Blank et al., 1978, 2003; van Kleeck et al., 2006). As you can see, *concrete thinking* involves tangible things you can see, hear, touch, or describe. In contrast, *abstract thinking* involves ideas beyond what you can observe to consider connections, patterns, and relationships, and to solve problems.

The science of reading makes it clear that abstract thinking is required to become a skilled reader. Level 3 questions (see page 90) focus on inferring, which requires students to use evidence in the text and reasoning skills to draw conclusions (Cain et al., 2001). Skilled readers do that because authors often leave out details that are needed to comprehend a text fully. Ask questions such as these to help students infer: "What might the character be thinking now?" or "Do you think this is a smart idea? Why or why not?" Learners also make inferences to build a richer picture of the text in their minds.

Level 4 questions focus on developing *causal reasoning*, a higher-level thinking skill that enables the reader to build knowledge by thinking about how text details affect one another. There are many forms of causal reasoning, such as understanding cause-and-effect relationships ("Why did this happen?"), considering what happens under various conditions ("What would happen if we changed...?"), and hypothesizing what made something happen ("How do you think they created...?") (Shavlik et al., 2022).

Recognize That Young Children Can Think Abstractly

Have you ever watched a toddler or preschooler examine how something works—like bubble wands or toy tools—and figure it out quickly? Research from the science and engineering fields shows that young children can reason at a higher level earlier than previously thought (Bonawitz et al., 2009; Guo et al., 2015; Greenfield et al., 2009; Sobel & Kirkham, 2006). For example, in an experiment where toddlers and preschoolers manipulated blocks to make a machine light up, researchers found they could use predictive inferences and causal reasoning to succeed (Bonawitz et al., 2009). Preschool-aged children required no assistance, but toddlers needed causal language from an adult. Specifically, when an adult drew the toddler's attention to the task by using Level 1 language, such as, "Look at my block. Here it goes!" it was not enough for the child to position the block to make the machine light up. But when the adult used Level 4 causal language such as, "The block makes the toy go. Can you make the toy go?" toddlers were successful. You can support this type of abstract thinking when your Strive-for-Five conversations focus on Level 3 and 4 types of questions.

Pushing Kids to Show What They Know With Strive-for-Five Conversations

Learning and displaying knowledge are valued in early childhood classrooms (van Kleeck et al., 2003). Strive-for-Five conversations allow you to differentiate support as you talk through students' ideas. This is important because while some students will come from home cultures that encourage them to display knowledge with family and friends, others won't. To differentiate instruction to address each student's needs, push for abstract thinking at turn 1 or turn 3 of the conversation.

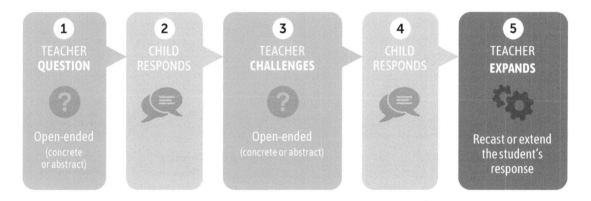

Your initial question in a Strive-for-Five conversation might be concrete or abstract, depending on the context, your learning goals, or the student's abilities and needs. For example, if you're at a place in a read-aloud where you want to check comprehension of an important point stated in the book, ask a concrete question. However, if you're focusing on science concepts, you might start with an abstract question to elicit higher-level reasoning. The third turn of Strive-for-Five conversation allows you to push for higher-level reasoning each time a student shows you he or she is correctly answering your first question. Or, if the child's response to the first question is incorrect or unclear, you may want to change your question to something more concrete or simple.

Inspire Learners From All Cultures to Show What They Know

Your students come from cultural backgrounds and home environments that vary in how children are socialized. Some families may not encourage children to demonstrate their knowledge by answering lots of questions. In fact, that behavior could be viewed unfavorably or as showing off (van Kleeck et al., 2003). Some children may be encouraged to tell stories at home or others may "show what they know" by pitching into family work or projects (Flood et al., 2004; Rogoff et al., 2015). Some children may rely heavily on nonverbal communication in their family's culture, rather than talking (Mejía-Arauz et al., 2012). So using gestures as you speak may be helpful. Strive-for-Five conversations allow you to gently encourage students to answer questions, even if that is something they don't typically do at home. Downward scaffolds during Strive-for-Five conversations can prevent uncomfortable situations where students feel they failed to demonstrate verbal reasoning because you stick with them and scaffold their responses, rather than turning to another student for a faster or more accurate response.

Examples of Conversations	
Only Turn 3 Pushes to Abstract	**Turns 1 and 3 Push to Abstract**
Strive-for-Five conversation during a read-aloud of an informational text on plants: **1** **TEACHER:** What are the parts of a plant? (concrete) **2** **STUDENT:** Plants have roots, a stem, and leaves. **3** **TEACHER:** That's right. Why do plants need roots under the ground? (abstract) **4** **STUDENT:** To help the plant stand up. **5** **TEACHER EXTENDS:** Yes, the roots hold the plant up and also give the plants water and nutrients.	Strive-for-Five conversation while checking growth of seeds children planted: **1** **TEACHER:** What if a seed does not have enough water? What do you think would happen? (abstract) **2** **STUDENT:** It would die. **3** **TEACHER:** Yes, without water, plants can die. If you give a plant like this water, what do you think would happen? (abstract) **4** **STUDENT:** It might be okay. **5** **TEACHER RESTATES:** It might be okay and survive or it may be too weak and die even though you tried to help.

Read-Aloud Questions That Build From Concrete to Abstract Reasoning

As you may recall from Chapter 3, we recommend asking questions before, during, and after read-alouds. Effective read-alouds often start by asking a "guiding question" to set a purpose for listening (Gonzalez et al., 2010; Wasik & Hindman, 2023; Zucker et al., 2019). If you pose a new guiding question each time you read a book aloud, you set a purpose for actively listening to the book again. Guiding questions are important questions that address an overarching idea in the text; they are previewed before reading and answered after reading with a series of Strive-for-Five conversations. There are many benefits to rereading books, such as increased exposure to new vocabulary as well as opportunities to push for abstract reasoning. If you reread books, you also don't have to "cram" too many questions into one read-aloud.

In addition to an overarching, guiding question, you can plan some stopping points to ask questions during reading. The chart on the next page shows various types of question stems that increase in complexity as you reread a book across multiple days (Zucker et al., 2019, 2021). There's evidence that gradually increasing the demand of questions as you reread books is an effective way to scaffold language comprehension because, as children become more familiar with the text, they can engage in higher-level reasoning about its concepts (Blewitt et al., 2009). Notice that the question stems used during reading are narrower and more specific than the stems for guiding questions. Of course, different books lend themselves to different types of questions. So, consider this a menu of question stems to select from to match the content in the book. Notice that this chart shows how you would reread a book three times with questions that become more challenging from Day 1 to Day 3.

Watch teachers ask guiding questions and use the Strive-for-Five framework to promote abstract thinking.

DAY 1: Initial Reading With Questions to Confirm Concrete Understanding	DAY 2: Reread With Questions to Push for Inferences	DAY 3: Reread With Questions to Push for More Abstract Reasoning

Before reading: Preview an important guiding question (GQ) to give students a purpose for listening to this book.

DAY 1: **Describing GQ**

- How were **characters in the text** ___ (traits, e.g., caring, etc.)?
- How does the character **solve the problem**?
- How do ____ (bunnies, plants, etc.) **change in the text**?
- What happened in the **beginning and end**?
- How can you tell this book is **informational** or a **narrative**?
- What topic/**category** of things are important to know to understand this text? (build **knowledge and schema**)

DAY 2: **Inferring GQ**

- How is ___ **similar** to/**different** from ___?
- How would you **compare**…?
- What is the **relationship/link between**…?
- How does ___ help/**support the character**?
- Why is ___ (event, e.g., dangerous, brave, other **opinion**, etc.)?
- How would **things be different if** ___?
- How does the **character become** ___ (smarter, famous, rich, etc.) in the text?

DAY 3: **Explaining GQ**

- **Why** is ____ (big issue) **important**?
- What is the **author's main point/** message?
- What **evidence** can you find to **explain** ___ (main idea)?
- What is a moral/**lesson learned** in this story?
- I wonder what **you learned** and what you're **still curious** about after reading about this (topic)?
- Why do you think these characters **solve the problem** in the way that they do and would you have done it **differently**?

During reading: Identify a few logical places during reading that warrant conversation, such as pivotal moments in the story or places where students can make an inference.

DAY 1: **Comprehension Checks**

- What is ___ doing? (name key **characters** and **events**)
- Where is this (event/story) taking place? (**setting**)
- What do you think will happen next? (**predict**) Was your prediction right?
- What do you notice about ___? (**describe**)
- What do you already know about ___? (**background knowledge**)
- What does ___ mean? (**define**)
- What is this object/thing made for/of? (define **purpose**)

DAY 2: **Key Inference Moments**

- How does the character feel about ___? (name **emotions**)
- What have you noticed so far about ___? (**patterns**)
- How is this similar to ___? (**compare**)
- How might this remind you of ___? (**connection**)
- What is the character thinking now? (name **cognition**)
- What does the character want? (name key **desires**)
- Do you think this is ___ (smart, useful, etc.) and why/why not? (explain your **opinion, judgment**)

DAY 3: **Causal Reasoning Checks**

- What do you think of how they solved this problem? (**reasoning**)
- I'm wondering about this ___ (event/illustration). Why do you think ___? (**explain details**)
- What are possible reasons ___? (**explain evidence**)
- Why did these things happen? (**cause/effect**)
- What questions do you still have about ___? (**summarize knowledge**)
- Reading this page makes me think the author…What do you think about ___? (**author purpose**)

After reading: Ask at least two students to answer an overarching GQ.

Avoid too many questions that interrupt the flow of reading to a point that distracts students. Pick logical stopping points and avoid questions that may lead to free association or rambling responses that have little to do with the text (Kintsch, 2005). Planning about six questions allows you to keep a good reading pace while listening to student reactions to the book. Routinely using guiding questions and equity sticks allow you to organize read-alouds in ways that benefit students (Cabell et al., 2019).

Use "Thinking Strategy" Posters

Consider using "Thinking Strategy" posters like the ones here to give students a nonverbal system to signal what they are thinking and what they want to contribute to the conversations. Introduce the posters by saying, "If you want to add to our conversation, you can show me the hand signal for the thinking strategy you plan to use." Then, as you engage in different read-alouds, you can reintroduce certain posters that are applicable. For example, when reading a book that requires inferring, direct students' attention to the "Make an Inference" poster and explain that authors usually do not connect all the dots in their books because they know that readers will make inferences on their own. Then point out when students do that: "You made a smart inference because you know that…" Encouraging nonverbal signals not only allows you to set the stage for conversations, but also gives students with limited language a way to express complex thinking without words.

Download the posters.

Unit Plans That Build From Concrete to Abstract

Instructional units are a series of lessons on a topic or theme that cross multiple curriculum areas (e.g., language arts, science, math). Let's consider how you can gradually push for abstract reasoning during a week-long instructional unit on growing plants. To introduce the unit, Ms. Jackson read aloud a book called *From Seed to Plant* by Gail Gibbons and asked the Day 1 guiding question, "What are the parts of plants?" During read-alouds later in the week, she pushed for more explanation of plant structure and function, as well as what plants need to survive. Rereading this expository text was an important part of this unit. She also read aloud other books on this topic and added books about plants to the classroom library to immerse students in these ideas. Chapter 7 provides examples of text sets that build student knowledge over time.

Ensure Multilingual Learners Show What They Know

English learners benefit, sometimes more than their monolingual peers, from Strive-for-Five conversations that support verbal reasoning (Silverman et al., 2020).

When students have learned about a topic in their home language, it is much easier for them to understand texts, vocabulary, and conversation about that topic in their second language (Cummins, 2017). When possible, you can bridge students' home language during conversations where this may help support complex reasoning because you translate key words or phrases. Even brief opportunities to translate and bridge to students' home language support verbal reasoning and text comprehension (Cummins, 2012; Fumero, 2022).

Small-group instruction is a great context to support verbal reasoning and other reading and writing skills because it allows you to tailor your instruction to the needs of students who are learning English (Gersten et al., 2007). Integrating the kinds of comprehension instruction and vocabulary instruction we describe in this book with decoding and reading and writing instruction is effective for many English learners (Solari et al., 2022); you may want to provide this type of integrated language and reading and writing instruction in small groups. This can be an efficient system to ensure your multilingual learners learn to understand increasingly complex texts while they are also building decoding skills (Baker et al., 2014).

Strive-for-Five conversations are perfect for supporting multilingual learners in English (Fumero, 2022) because they include open-ended questioning paired with language-support strategies such as direct vocabulary instruction, recasting, or extending student responses. Chapter 5 talks about explicit vocabulary instruction, and Chapter 8 provides details on recasting and extending student responses.

Small-Group Work During the Unit

These interactive read-alouds set the stage for small-group explorations of how seeds grow. With groups of four to five students, Ms. Jackson reviewed key vocabulary words about plants and had multiple Strive-for-Five conversations with students, using a series of activities that required increasingly abstract thinking across the week (e.g., Day 1: Monday, Day 2: Wednesday, and Day 3: Friday).

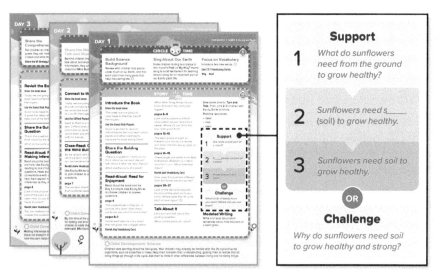

Suggested Scaffold for Strive-for-Five Turn 3

Support

1. *What do sunflowers need from the ground to grow healthy?*

2. *Sunflowers need s_____ (soil) to grow healthy.*

3. *Sunflowers need soil to grow healthy.*

OR

Challenge

Why do sunflowers need soil to grow healthy and strong?

DAY 1: Build Background Knowledge	DAY 2: Explain Reasoning	DAY 3: Infer Outcomes
Which of these are pictures of "living things" or "nonliving things"? Let's sort them into two groups.	What order should these pictures be in to show how a plant grows? Let's talk about the stages in a plant's life cycle as we put these in order.	How can you take care of plants to help them grow? Let's act out plant care activities. Let's also imagine what could happen if plants did not get these kinds of care.

Students planted their own seeds in a clear cup of dirt. The teacher asked them to use their scientist notebook (a spiral notebook they used throughout the year to record observations and gather data) to draw and write about how their seeds were growing over time. Young children cannot make inferences that support comprehension unless they have prior knowledge of the words and concepts (Cain, 2022; Diprossimo et al., 2023). So you may need to provide information and hints to guide students' learning. During read-alouds and small-group activities, flip back to pages or point out observable evidence that's necessary for making an accurate inference (Cain, 2022).

Writing That Builds From Concrete to Abstract

Another way to nurture abstract thinking after a read-aloud is to encourage students to draw and write about the text. In these photos, Ms. Carr is encouraging her first graders to think about *Happy Birthday, Moon* by Frank Asch, a book they read and discussed. The guiding question she kicked off the read-aloud with was, "What would you like to give the moon for its birthday? Why?" After reading the book, Ms. Carr and her students are finally ready to answer the guiding question. Ms. Carr asked about three students to answer the guiding question in the whole-group setting, using the Strive-for-Five approach to scaffold their verbal responses. Then she encouraged all to answer the guiding question via drawing and writing. She said, "I love your imaginations! Now I want to see what birthday present each of you would give the moon, like Bear. So, please go to your desks to draw and write about this question."

Watch teachers ask guiding questions and use the Strive-for-Five framework to promote abstract thinking.

This student's answer to the guiding question was, "I would give the moon 500 bucks," and Ms. Carr pushed him to explain why, using the Strive-for-Five approach. He described how that was a lot of money and could probably buy the moon anything he wanted. So, she encouraged him to extend his writing.

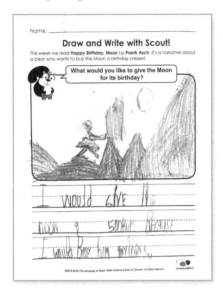

Ms. Carr had a Strive-for-Five conversation with the student who wrote the response on the right about his writing:

1 **STUDENT:** Ms. Carr, can I show you mine? I wrote, "I would give the moon a basketball so when it is daytime the moon can play. When it's dark, the moon can play with the sun."

2 **MS. CARR (concrete question):** Wow, this is very creative. Where is the basketball in your drawing?

3 **STUDENT:** It's here. [Student points to center circle.]

4 **MS. CARR (abstract question):** I see. Where do you think you would draw Earth if you added it to this picture?

5 **STUDENT:** I'm not sure. I think it might be in between them.

6 **MS. CARR:** Yes, that would make sense. You could do a little more research if you want. You can go to the computer center and search for a NASA video about day and night on the moon so you can learn more about what it is like on the moon at different times and add onto your message.

Notice how Ms. Carr moved the conversation from concrete to abstract topics, while encouraging the child to do more research and writing.

Final Word: Challenge Students by Asking Abstract Reasoning Questions

Encourage young children to show what they know by moving Strive-for-Five conversations from concrete topics to abstract ones. Doing that builds the higher-level thinking skills they need to succeed in school. Planning questions for repeated read-alouds of a book and across instructional units allows you to push for higher-level reasoning. When you ask questions that are challenging for students, this gives you an opportunity to scaffold and guide learning. Combining those types of language comprehension supports with vocabulary instruction appears to be the most effective way to ensure positive reading outcomes (Silverman et al., 2020).

Reflect and Implement

How can you push your students to show what they know during Strive-for-Five conversations? How can you move them toward more abstract talk?

Brainstorm two guiding questions that push students' thinking, based on a book you read aloud to them recently.

How can you use your curricular materials to promote abstract reasoning?

What writing prompts might you use to encourage students to show what they know?

CHAPTER 7

Did You Know?

Conversations Build Knowledge

Mr. Fazal is reading aloud the informational book *From Seed to Plant* by Gail Gibbons to his first graders—one of four books he is using to teach them about the life cycle of plants. His goal is to deepen students' knowledge of that topic not only through listening to the book, but also through Strive-for-Five conversations about the book.

After reading it, Mr. Fazal reminds students of the question he asked them to think about before the read-aloud.

1 **MR. FAZAL:** How does a plant change as it grows?

2 **KENNY:** It gets bigger.

3 MR. FAZAL: Yes, a plant does grow bigger. Tell me more about that.

4 KENNY: It starts as a tiny seed. And then it grows.

5 MR. FAZAL: Do you remember the word for when a seed starts to grow?

6 KENNY: Germination!

7 MR. FAZAL: Yes, the seed germinates. Then how does the plant change?

Notice how Mr. Fazal builds students' knowledge of the life cycle of plants, while strengthening their oral language. He continues the conversation on the topic well beyond five turns, and his students are engaged in the topic as they discuss key ideas and advanced vocabulary words.

Mr. Fazal knows that it takes time for knowledge to develop, so he gives his students coherent content learning experiences. For example, in addition to this read-aloud, he immerses his students in science investigations that involve

Terms to Know

Background Knowledge is the information a reader or listener has about topics in the text. It also includes the information that a person brings into conversations.

Content Knowledge includes knowledge of the natural and social world (often science and social studies topics). It is sometimes considered a subcategory of background knowledge.

Imaginative Play is a form of play in which a child pretends to be someone or somewhere else by role-playing or taking another's perspective.

Inquiry-Based Learning is a form of learning in which students are asked to figure out a solution to a problem or explore a concept, based on a question or series of questions.

Integrated Content and Literacy Instruction infuses content-area teaching into literacy instruction or infuses literacy instruction into content-area teaching. Both literacy and content knowledge are focal points of instruction.

A **Schema** is the way we organize and connect knowledge in the brain about a topic or domain.

Situation Model is the third level of comprehension that is the overall mental model created by bringing to bear background knowledge to understanding the textbase.

Surface Level is the first level of comprehension where we are able to read the words on the page, even if we don't quite understand them.

Textbase is the second level of comprehension that includes understanding how the text is structured (macrostructure) and the individual ideas and how they connect to each other (microstructure).

planting seeds and observing plants grow. He also knows that teaching about the life cycle of plants will help him build his students' knowledge about other types of life cycles (e.g., insects, frogs).

Why Knowledge Matters for Language Comprehension

The background knowledge strand in Scarborough's Rope is an important component of language comprehension. *Background knowledge* is required to understand what we are listening to or reading. It helps us make inferences and fill in gaps in a text. Background knowledge is essential to reading and listening for understanding (Cromley & Azevedo, 2007; Kintsch, 1998; Stafura & Perfetti, 2017).

How does our background knowledge help us to comprehend? As we listen to or read a text, we comprehend at three levels: surface level, textbase level, and the situation model (Kintsch, 1998; Student Achievement Partners, 2021).

> The *surface* level is being able to read the words on the page, even if we don't quite understand them.
>
> The *textbase* level includes understanding the macrostructure and microstructure of the text. The macrostructure is how the text is structured (e.g., setting, characters, problem, solution). The microstructure includes the individual ideas and how they connect to each other.
>
> The *situation model* is the overall mental model created by bringing to bear background knowledge to understanding the textbase. We use our own relevant knowledge to fill in gaps and make inferences, leading to a deeper understanding of the text.

To help students create a situation model during an interactive read-aloud, it's important to first activate their background knowledge of the topic. You can

Strike Up Conversations During Science

A natural time for Strive-for-Five conversations is during content-area instruction, particularly science instruction (Cabell, DeCoster, et al., 2013). In a sample of 314 preschool teachers from across the United States, we examined teacher-child interactions across various points in the day, including read-aloud, literacy, math, science, social studies, and art/music. We found that during science (as compared to other points in the day), teachers did a better job promoting higher-order thinking, providing feedback, and modeling formal language structures, which suggests that a great time to strike up Strive-for-Five conversations may be when students are engaged in science activities such as investigations, observations, and informational text read-alouds.

do that by asking questions about the text you're about to read or reminding students of prior learning related to the topic.

But we can't assume students have the knowledge they need to comprehend the text. So, we need to do more than "activate" their knowledge. We need to *build* it—specifically, their *content knowledge*: their knowledge about the natural and social world. In other words, teaching science and social studies topics systematically is important for building the rich store of knowledge students will need not only in the early grades, but also in Grade 3 and beyond.

Building Content Knowledge to Boost Language Comprehension

In the United States, building content knowledge is not always a priority in the elementary grades (Tyner & Kabourek, 2021). Many teachers spend a lot of time on reading and writing instruction and less on content-area instruction. This might be due to the fact that traditional English Language Arts curriculum materials—even high-quality materials—aren't usually designed to build content knowledge (Paige et al., 2021). They are usually designed to build literacy. Therefore, materials aren't typically connected to content-area topics, so they may activate students' knowledge but not build it. Creators of those materials may wrongly assume that robust content-area instruction is going on during the school day.

We need to build content knowledge in science and social studies topics from preschool on up! Otherwise, students may have difficulties understanding the texts you read aloud and, in time, texts they read on their own. They may encounter challenges in reading when they reach the upper elementary grades and are expected to read about and understand all kinds of topics. So they must arrive prepared with as much background knowledge as possible.

Integrate Content and Literacy Instruction

One way to build students' content knowledge while strengthening their language skills is to use *integrated content and literacy instruction*, which means either infusing content-area teaching into literacy instruction or infusing literacy teaching into content-area instruction. Doing that not only builds students' background knowledge, but also strengthens their vocabulary and reading comprehension (Hwang, Cabell, et al., 2022, 2023).

What does integrated content and literacy instruction look like in the early grades? And where do Strive-for-Five conversations fit in? We devote the rest of this chapter to answering those questions.

These instructional practices are hallmarks of integrated content and literacy instruction (Hwang et al., 2021). By embracing them, you will be well on your way to building your students' knowledge in a big way.

- Plan instructional units around science and social studies topics.
- Provide content-rich read-alouds using text sets that build knowledge.
- Focus discussions and writing on building knowledge.
- Teach relationships between and among words.
- Build knowledge during guided play.

Plan Instructional Units Around Science and Social Studies Topics

Plan instructional units around science and/or social studies topics, with knowledge building as a chief aim of instruction. As noted in Chapter 6, *instructional units* are a series of lessons that address a topic or theme across multiple curriculum areas. Select content topics based on standards and curriculum requirements, and sequence them so they make sense to students and build their knowledge systematically. Unit length varies, but around two weeks per topic works for most teachers we know.

In our research on effective integrated content and literacy approaches, we have seen a variety of unit topics (Cabell & Hwang, 2020; Hwang, Cabell, et al., 2022, 2023). Here are just a few examples:

PreK: Insects, Marine Mammals, Places We Live and Go, Earth—Land and Water (Gonzalez et al., 2010; Neuman & Kaefer, 2018b)

Kindergarten: Farms, Plants, Transportation, Observation Using the Five Senses, Seasons & Weather (Core Knowledge Foundation & Amplify Education, 2017; Connor et al., 2017)

First Grade: Goods and Services, Animal Survival, Living and Nonliving Things, Earth's Surface, Phases of Matter, Pushes and Pulls (Connor et al., 2017; Kim et al., 2023; Vitale & Romance, 2012)

Some approaches consider how topics are introduced within a school year and across school years. For example, one curriculum introduces plants to kindergartners, so they have some background knowledge before it introduces them to farms (Core Knowledge Foundation & Amplify, 2017). Curricula may also spiral content teaching by revisiting and deepening a topic over years (Kim & Burkhauser, 2022). In that way, students can actively use the content that you have taught as background knowledge when they read or listen to a new text.

Teach Schemas for Long-Term Positive Effects

A schema is the way we organize and connect knowledge in the brain about a particular topic or domain. It is constantly changing as we learn new things. You might think of it like a spider web—when our schema about a topic is well structured, we can "catch" new knowledge. We use our existing schemas to understand and learn from the texts we read or listen to.

You can also think of a schema as a tree and its branches (Kim & Burkhauser, 2022). The diagram below shows that a schema could be "houses" (tree), the foundational knowledge could be "what houses look like" (trunk), and the branches represent topic knowledge about what various types of houses look like on the inside (e.g., ranch-style house, apartment, townhouse, wigwam, igloo). The leaves on the tree represent how much one knows about the particular topic.

In this example, you can see how being knowledgeable about a familiar house might help you understand a passage about a less familiar house, such as an igloo or wigwam. With a broad schema, students are more likely transfer knowledge to many topics (Kim et al., 2023).

Kim and Burkhauser (2022) describe the power of building content knowledge by explicitly teaching schemas over time. They show that content-rich reading and writing instruction, based on teaching schemas to first graders through third graders, has long-term positive effects on reading comprehension (Kim, Burkhauser, et al., 2023; Kim, Gilbert, et al., 2023). Using a general schema of living systems, first graders learned about animal survival. In second grade, they built on that knowledge by learning how scientists study animal extinction. In third grade, they continued to build schema by learning about systems of the human body.

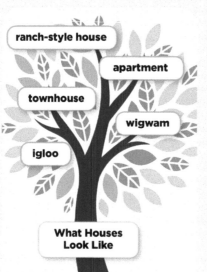

ranch-style house

apartment

townhouse

wigwam

igloo

What Houses Look Like

Provide Content-Rich Read-Alouds Using Text Sets That Build Knowledge

Select sets of texts around a theme or topic that are designed to deepen content knowledge over successive readings, and contain recurring vocabulary words and concepts (Wright et al., 2022). Consider a range of genres, including informational and narrative (Neuman & Kaefer, 2018a). These conceptually coherent text sets ensure that children are exposed to repeated and related words and ideas to build knowledge. Furthermore, because texts we read aloud to children are often much more complex than texts they can read on their own, we also expose them to advanced language structures. The box below features example text sets for a unit entitled "Our Earth." Each book deepens students' knowledge of the planet.

"Our Earth" Text Sets for Read-Alouds

PreK

- *Happy Birthday, Moon* by Frank Asch (narrative, discuss objects in the sky)
- *Rainy, Sunny, Blowy, Snowy* by Jane Brocket (informational, discuss the earth's weather patterns)
- *Agua, Agüita/ Water, Little Water* by Jorge Tetl Argueta (informational, discuss the earth's elements)
- *The Earth Book* by Todd Parr (informational, discuss taking care of our environment)

Grade K

- *Seeds! Seeds! Seeds!* by Nancy Elizabeth Wallace (narrative, discuss how seeds grow)
- *Seed, Soil, Sun* by Cris Peterson (informational, discuss how the food we eat germinates and grows)
- *Amazing Plant Powers* by Loreen Leedy and Andrew Schuerger (informational, discuss plant parts and functions)
- *It's Our Garden: From Seeds to Harvest in a School Garden* by George Ancona (informational, discuss the plants in a school garden)

continued on next page

"Our Earth" Text Sets for Read-Alouds *continued*

Grade 1

- *Protecting Earth's Waters* (Learn About: Water) by Cody Crane (informational, discuss the importance of water on Earth)
- *The Ocean Is Kind of a Big Deal* by Nick Seluk (dual-purpose, discuss how oceans positively contribute to the world)
- *Life in a Coral Reef* by Wendy Pfeffer (informational, discuss the importance of coral reefs)
- *Ocean Sunlight* by Molly Bang and Penny Chisholm (dual-purpose, discuss how the sun is critical to the food chains in the ocean)

Focus Discussions and Writing on Building Knowledge

One of the best ways to support knowledge building is not only by engaging in content-rich read-alouds, but also engaging children in discussions before, during, and after those read-alouds. When you discuss a book, in addition to reading it, you help to improve children's vocabulary (Zucker et al., 2013). As detailed in Chapter 6, by asking concrete questions (e.g., Why do plants need water to survive?) and abstract questions (e.g., What do you think happens when a plant doesn't get water?), you encourage active participation by giving children opportunities to discuss their ideas.

Let's revisit Mr. Fazal's classroom to see how he asks questions to encourage student participation. After the read-aloud of *From Seed to Plant*, he continues a Strive-for-Five conversation with Kenny about the life cycle of plants.

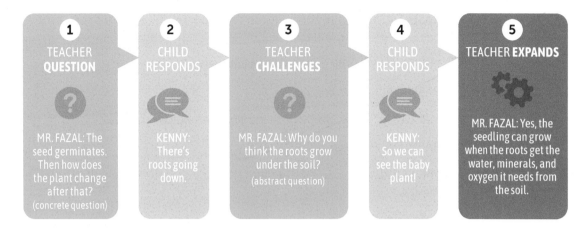

1 TEACHER **QUESTION**	2 CHILD RESPONDS	3 TEACHER **CHALLENGES**	4 CHILD RESPONDS	5 TEACHER **EXPANDS**
MR. FAZAL: The seed germinates. Then how does the plant change after that? (concrete question)	KENNY: There's roots going down.	MR. FAZAL: Why do you think the roots grow under the soil? (abstract question)	KENNY: So we can see the baby plant!	MR. FAZAL: Yes, the seedling can grow when the roots get the water, minerals, and oxygen it needs from the soil.

In addition to Strive-for-Five conversations around read-alouds, you can build knowledge during inquiry-based STEM activities, such as observing how seeds grow into plants or mixing colored water drops to create a new color. Your conversations will build content knowledge and verbal reasoning skills (French, 2004; Vartiainen & Kumpulainen, 2020). It is often easier to develop abstract thinking about concepts during science than other subjects, perhaps even easier than during read-alouds (Hadley & Mendez, 2021). That is because science is so content rich and emphasizes *inquiry-based learning*, in which teachers give students hands-on materials and ask them to solve a problem or explore a concept. Still, we often find that young children need Strive-for-Five conversations to form accurate conclusions and consider important, crosscutting concepts in STEM (National Research Council, 2012).

Mr. Fazal engages his students in Strive-for-Five conversations during inquiry-based learning. He is careful to pay attention to the questions students ask and uses them as starting points for conversations. Allowing students to ask questions is an important way to foster their learning (Chouinard et al., 2007). Starting with their questions can be powerful (Kurkul et al., 2022).

The students in Mr. Fazal's class plant seeds in clear plastic cups. Each day, they write down their observations in their science notebooks, noting how the plant changes as it grows. Mr. Fazal responds to his student Rashida's question.

1 **RASHIDA:** What are all these lines? (pointing to the roots that have started to grow along the side of the cup)

2 **MR. FAZAL:** What do you think those lines are?

3 RASHIDA: Well, it is coming from the soil. I don't think it's the plant because it's not green.

4 MR. FAZAL: Are all parts of the plant green?

5 RASHIDA: I don't know.

6 MR. FAZAL: What part of the plant grows below the soil?

7 RASHIDA: (shrugs)

8 MR. FAZAL: The part of the plant that grows below the soil is called the rrr....

9 RASHIDA: Roots!

10 MR. FAZAL: The roots help the plant to grow.

In this photo, you can see another teacher, Dr. Fumero, engage preschoolers in extended conversations about seeds they planted, part of a unit of study called "Caring for Plants."

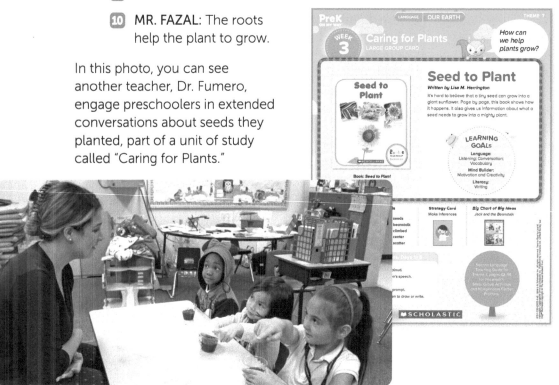

Integrated content and literacy instruction also include writing that supports knowledge building. For example, you might have students draw and write responses related to the read-aloud on topics such as plant care, plants as food, or plants of various ecosystems (desert, rainforest).

The chart below shows how Dr. Fumero asked children to draw and write about increasingly complex ideas in their science notebooks. Also note that she started preparing for this unit weeks beforehand and had planted her own clear cups with seeds so students could see different stages of the plant life cycle. She also had taped to the window clear plastic bags with wet paper towels and seeds at a few different stages of germination. Each small group conducted an experiment where they placed Dr. Fumero's cup with seeds in an unusual place—for example, one was in a dark closet and another was far from the window near students' backpacks. Over time, this allowed students to see how the seeds placed in darker spots did not get enough light.

Watch knowledge-building conversations about seeds students planted as part of a unit of study called "Caring for Plants."

Notebook Questions That Build Knowledge and Push for Inferences

DAY 1: Questions to Confirm Concrete Understanding	DAY 2: Questions to Push for Comparison	DAY 3: Questions to Push for Inferences
Observe the different plants in our window. Draw a plant with parts above the ground and below the ground.	Go to the window and draw how your seed looks today. Look at the seeds in the clear bags that started growing earlier. Draw those seeds also. What is different about these seeds?	Go to the window to observe your seed. Then go find your group's seed that we placed away from the window. How are they different? What things does your seed need to grow?

Teach Relationships Between and Among Words

Select vocabulary words to teach explicitly. Be sure to not only define the words in child-friendly language, but also to teach conceptual relationships between and among them. For example, you might define *seed* as containing a tiny plant that will grow into a large plant and *germinate* as when the seed begins to break open (sprout) as the tiny plant grows. But don't stop there! Give an example that it's "necessary for a seed to germinate in order for it to sprout."

Teaching words in categories can be powerful for children's learning (Neuman et al., 2011, 2021; Neuman & Kaefer, 2018a and 2018b). For example, leaves, roots, stems, flowers, fruits, and seeds are all parts of a plant. Whales, manatees, and dolphins are all marine mammals and belong to the larger class of wild animals. Teaching vocabulary this way allows children to create more coherent networks of knowledge.

Use high-quality, content-rich curricula—materials, resources, and lessons—to guide your instruction. While some school districts have developed their own curricula, there are knowledge-building reading and writing curricula available that embrace the practices we recommend in this chapter. For example, the chart below captures words and connections between words that are taught in a preschool unit entitled "Our Earth."

Build Knowledge During Play

Consider Strive-for-Five conversations during *imaginative play*, in which a child pretends to be someone else or somewhere else, because it, too, lends itself to asking abstract questions that require higher-level thinking (Lillard et al., 2013). When children imagine themselves in different roles and transport themselves to imaginary places, they assume the personalities and perspectives of others, which requires abstract reasoning. For example, the graphic on the next page shows a weeklong preschool unit designed to teach students about plants. Notice how it includes conversation prompts and playful ideas to build knowledge, such as making plant costumes at the pretend and learn center, and building something as tall as a sunflower at the construction center.

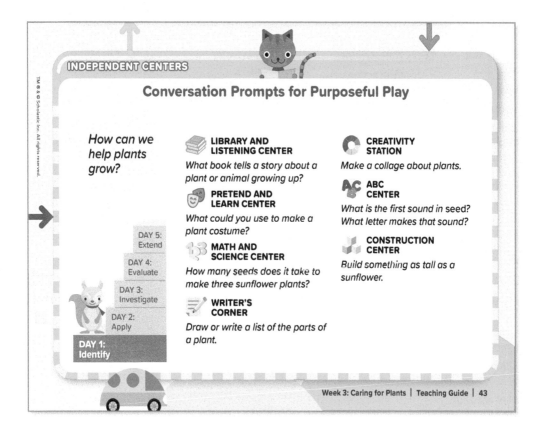

INDEPENDENT CENTERS

Conversation Prompts for Purposeful Play

How can we help plants grow?

DAY 5: Extend
DAY 4: Evaluate
DAY 3: Investigate
DAY 2: Apply
DAY 1: Identify

LIBRARY AND LISTENING CENTER
What book tells a story about a plant or animal growing up?

PRETEND AND LEARN CENTER
What could you use to make a plant costume?

MATH AND SCIENCE CENTER
How many seeds does it take to make three sunflower plants?

WRITER'S CORNER
Draw or write a list of the parts of a plant.

CREATIVITY STATION
Make a collage about plants.

ABC CENTER
What is the first sound in seed? What letter makes that sound?

CONSTRUCTION CENTER
Build something as tall as a sunflower.

Week 3: Caring for Plants | Teaching Guide | 43

During imaginative play enhanced with reading and writing activities, individualize support by switching up materials to make a task easier or more challenging (Copp et al., 2023). For example, you can scaffold downward with hand-over-hand support to write a letter when a preschooler needs physical support. Alternatively, you can scaffold upward by encouraging children to gather data by writing (e.g., tallies or sorting) during their play. One of our favorite ways to make play more challenging is to have students create lists, invitations, signs, and other authentic forms of written communication (Neuman & Roskos, 1993). The chart on the next page shows how to integrate Strive-for-Five conversations and scaffolding during knowledge-building activities.

Scaffolding Moves During Guided Play to Build Knowledge and Verbal Reasoning

CONCRETE ← → ABSTRACT

LEVEL 1: Naming and Physical Assistance

- Name objects
- Narrate actions
- Provide hand-over-hand scaffolds where you help guide a child's hand with an object or writing tool
- Give, objects, tools, or options to make a task simpler

Examples:

- *You are using the…*
- *I see you can move the…*
- *Let's move it, write it, push it together…*
- *Let's try this one that is easier to…*
- *Find another one that matches…*

LEVEL 2: Describing

- Describe actions and movements
- Point and gesture during play
- Point to pictures and visual aids
- Give one-step instructions

Examples:

- *I noticed you are doing that fast/slow, carefully, etc.*
- *Look at this one.*
- *Do you want to try…*
- *Which group does this belong in?*

LEVEL 3: Planning and Retelling

- Use a visual schedule or steps
- Plan for future steps
- Give instructions in 2–3 steps
- Name feelings and emotions by guessing what the child's non-verbal signals or facial expressions show
- Give objects, tools, or options to make a task more challenging
- Give feedback about good choices
- Retell and review play events

Examples:

- *Let's review our center rotation…*
- *The first thing to do is… and then you…*
- *What do you plan to work on at the… center?*
- *I can see you're feeling excited about…*
- *Looks like you're getting frustrated…*
- *That was a smart idea to…*

LEVEL 4: Reasoning and Problem-Solving

- Explain why things happened
- Use language to think aloud about solving problems
- Set up multi-step experiments increasingly led by students

Examples:

- *Why do you think…?*
- *How can we fix…?*
- *What do you want to try to…?*
- *This will take a few days, but first you can… then, tomorrow you might…*

Final Word: Engage Students in Content-Rich Strive-for-Five Conversations

Your day is filled with opportunities for Strive-for-Five conversations that build students' science and social studies knowledge. But conversations alone are not enough. We always need to be sure they are on topics that inspire our students' curiosity (Jirout, 2020). We can integrate content and literacy instruction through thoughtful read-alouds of conceptually coherent texts, discussion of vocabulary while deepening students' knowledge of the topic, and conversations throughout the day that nurture curiosity and support language comprehension.

Reflect and Implement

- How do you build your students' background knowledge?
- Think about your conversations with students over the past few days. Describe one you had about a science or social studies topic. Did it promote vocabulary discussion, building knowledge, or abstract thinking?
- What are some challenges you face when trying to implement content-rich, Strive-for-Five conversations in the classroom?
- Create a conceptually coherent text set on a topic of your choice using four books. You may want to consider using narrative and informational genres. How does each book deepen students' knowledge of the topic?

CHAPTER 8

Build on What They Say!

Modeling Formal Language Structures

Mrs. Rodriguez just finished reading aloud *I Get Wet* by Vicki Cobb to her first-grade class as part of a unit on properties of matter. She asks an open-ended question to get students thinking about the differences between liquids and solids.

1 **MRS. RODRIGUEZ:** Water is a liquid. What is a characteristic of a liquid that makes it different from a solid?

2 **NIA:** Water is different than ice.

3 **MRS. RODRIGUEZ:** Yes, water is a liquid, and it is different from ice, the solid form of water. How are water and ice different?

4 **NIA:** The boy poured the water into the pan. And it fitted it.

5 **MRS. RODRIGUEZ:** When the boy poured water into the pan, the water fit into the pan. Liquid takes the shape of its container. Let's look again at that page in the book...

In this Strive-for-Five conversation, Mrs. Rodriguez not only builds Nia's science knowledge, but also models formal language structures. Without breaking the flow of ideas, she models conventional grammar in mainstream American English in the fifth turn by rephrasing the child's response. In the same turn, Mrs. Rodriguez also extends Nia's idea.

The fifth turn in a Strive-for-Five conversation provides an opportunity to model complex syntax or ideas by rephrasing and building on the child's message. During whole-class conversations, this can benefit all students. This chapter explains why modeling formal language structures is important to students' developing language comprehension—and shows you how to do it.

Why Language Structures Matter for Reading

To read and write successfully, children need to understand and use formal language structures at the word, sentence, and passage levels. Spoken language and written language are quite different from one another. Spoken language, including everyday conversations, is generally delivered in an informal register. Written language, including the language of most books children encounter at school, is delivered in a formal register, full of complex language structures (Foorman et al., 2016).

Strive-for-Five conversations can advance children's understanding of advanced language at the word, sentence, and conversation levels (Barnes et al., 2021). As children's understanding of written language grows, they move toward a literate language style (Paul, 1995), which they develop as they progress in school (Pence

Terms to Know

Conventional Grammar is the agreed-upon rules of accepted usage of a given language, including syntax. In this book, we use the term to refer to mainstream American English.

Extending a child's message means building on it by providing more information or explanation, or prompting the child to say more.

Language Structures refers to how we combine words to craft sentences, including grammatical rules (e.g., syntax) and how word choice affects meaning (e.g., semantics).

Recasting a child's message means restructuring it in a way that makes it more syntactically accurate.

et al., 2008). They begin to understand and use complex syntax that doesn't occur frequently in everyday conversations but does in written language. For example, we might read the following sentence, but not say it:

"Because Jan's book was overdue, she drove to the library to return it."

Early exposure to the language of books is important for children's literacy development. Children need to hear formal language structures and engage in conversations in which they use this formal language. Interactive read-alouds offer an excellent context for them to hear and use formal language structures in Strive-for-Five conversations. Even young children show that they can understand and use these structures after hearing them modeled (Huttenlocher et al., 2004).

How we use language with our students affects their understanding of language. When teacher talk is syntactically complex, students come to understand complex language more deeply (Huttenlocher et al., 2002). When responding to something a teacher says, children tend to mirror his or her syntax (Justice et al., 2013). In other words, children may use more formal language structures with a teacher than with peers. This highlights the importance of sticking to the topic during Strive-for-Five conversations.

Honor and Build From Dialect

You probably have students who are bidialectal, meaning that they speak more than one variety of English (Wolfram & Schilling-Estes, 2006). For example, a student may speak mainstream American English and African American English, or mainstream American English and Southern American English. When teachers view bidialectalism as a language difference, like multilingualism, and not as a deficit, students can develop strong reading and writing skills (Terry et al., 2018). Keep in mind, though, those with a high dialect density—when students use a dialect in more than half of what they say—may need more models of formal language structures to help them access the language used in books and at school (Washington & Seidenberg, 2021). There are key differences in language structures between mainstream American English and other English dialects. For example, in African American English, a student might say, "She be gettin' a pet," or "He smart." You can recast what a student is saying using a model in mainstream American English by saying, "Oh, she is getting a pet! How fun," or "Yes, he is smart!" But it is important to avoid communicating to students that they are speaking incorrectly. Simply respond to a student's message, while providing a language model.

How to Model Formal Language Structures

Through conversations, you can model formal language structures for children without distracting them from the topic under discussion. We discuss two strategies in this section—recast and extend—which you can use at any conversation turn. But, during whole-class and small-group instruction, we have noticed teachers use them at the fifth turn of a Strive-for-Five conversation to end by giving voice to an individual student's key idea, while allowing all students to listen and absorb important aspects of the conversation.

Strategy 1: Recast

When you recast a child's message, you restructure it in a way that makes it more syntactically correct (Nelson et al., 1996), which provides the child with feedback on a language structure that he or she has not yet mastered (Cleave et al., 2015). Recasting is a type of downward scaffold to use when a student makes a grammatical or syntactic error.

> **STUDENT:** I goed to the farm and saw two sheeps.
>
> **TEACHER:** Wow, you went to the farm and saw two sheep?
>
> **STUDENT:** I winned the game.
>
> **TEACHER:** Congratulations! You won the game!

In the example above, a teacher might be tempted to say, "No, you won the game. Say it correctly, 'I won the game.'" However, asking the child to repeat after you detracts from the conversation, and children don't need to repeat it after you to learn from your model (Nelson et al., 1996). There's no need to explain details of the error, such as "That's an irregular past tense verb, so you say 'went' instead of 'goed.'" In fact, you will likely lose young students' attention when you offer unnecessary explanations.

Strategy 2: Extend

You can extend a child's contribution to a conversation by building on it with more information or explanation about an object, action, or topic. Extending is a form of upward scaffolding because the teacher adds onto or responds to the child's already accurate message. An extension should always build on the child's focus and respond to the child's interests. The child should be inspired to think about what he or she just said. You can extend a child's message to make it more semantically complex (Justice et al., 2018). To do that, at your turn in the conversation, repeat the child's message but extend the idea by adding a word, phrase, or more explanation to make it longer. This is a "mirror plus," or a reflection of the child's message, plus language that increases its complexity and makes students think (Girolametto et al., 2000).

In this example, the teacher adds a word:

>STUDENT: A mouse!

>TEACHER: A tiny mouse.

Here the teacher adds a phrase:

>STUDENT: Look at that big fish.

>TEACHER: Look at that big fish swimming in the water.

In these two examples, the teacher provides a vocabulary word and an idea to the message:

>STUDENT: Write my words.

>TEACHER: You want me to write down your story so you can read it back later.

>STUDENT: Mark gets two crackers and I get two.

>TEACHER: You're dividing the crackers equally.

In these three examples, the teacher extends the child's message by providing even more information and explanation:

>STUDENT: Baby is eating.

>TEACHER: The baby is eating food so that her bones can grow until she is big and strong, just like you!

>STUDENT: It's snowing.

>TEACHER: It is snowing, so we have to wear hats and gloves to keep our head and hands warm.

>STUDENT: It's still raining.

>TEACHER: You're right. It's still raining. The schoolyard will be too wet, so we won't be able to go out for recess today.

You don't have to repeat or rephrase what the child says. You can keep the conversation going by prompting the child to say more, by asking questions that tap into his or her interests.

> STUDENT: Fifty dollars.
>
> TEACHER: Where do you think I can get fifty dollars?
>
> STUDENT: All her doors are locked.
>
> TEACHER: All her doors are locked, but what could happen if the wolf came in?

When you extend the child's message, you are building students' language comprehension. Whether you are adding one word to describe the color, size, shape, or texture of something, or adding more information to the child's message, you are continuing the conversation and, therefore, developing the child's language structures, verbal reasoning, and background knowledge. (See Chapter 6 for more on verbal reasoning and Chapter 7 for more on building knowledge.)

Support Multilingual Learners With English Language Structures

Multilingual learners benefit from the strategies we explain in this chapter. Keep in mind, though, they may need additional supports to develop a strong grasp of English language structures (Fumero, 2022). Those supports include bridging and teaching cognates, both discussed in Chapter 5.

Extend Talk During Guided Play

Here are excerpts from conversations in a preschool classroom, where students and their teacher were working with Play-Doh in a small group. The column on the left shows the students' initial comments and the teacher's responses. The column on the right shows ways the teacher could extend what the students said by adding a phrase or idea.

Classroom Conversation	Possible Extension
STUDENT: I'm cutting. TEACHER: Good job. Good cutting.	STUDENT: I'm cutting. TEACHER: You are cutting the Play-Doh with a knife.
STUDENT: I did it, Ms. Jones! TEACHER: Good job.	STUDENT: I did it, Ms. Jones! TEACHER: You flattened the Play-Doh like a pancake.
STUDENT: I'm cutting a banana. TEACHER: Oh, you're cutting a banana.	STUDENT: I'm cutting a banana. TEACHER: You're cutting your banana to put in your banana pudding.

Use Extensions to Promote Vocabulary Learning

Provide a new word: During Strive-for-Five conversations, you could introduce the student to a new word.

1 **SEBASTIAN:** I don't like going to the dentist.

2 **MR. CORTEZ:** When I don't know what might happen somewhere, I feel *nervous*. I might be *nervous* to go to the dentist because I don't know what might happen there. Do you feel *nervous*?

3 **SEBASTIAN:** Yes.

4 **MR. CORTEZ:** How do you feel about going to the dentist?

5 **SEBASTIAN:** I feel **NERVOUS**.

Provide more information about a word: You can also provide more information about a word a student uses to deepen knowledge about it.

1 **MRS. LITTLE:** Do you remember what happened when we went on our field trip to the zoo last month?

2 **MARK:** We took a detour.

3 **MRS. LITTLE:** You're right! Our school bus had to take a *detour*. We had to find another way to get there. Why did we have to take a detour?

4 **MARK:** Because the road was blocked.

5 **MRS. LITTLE:** Yes, the road was blocked because of construction. So we took a *detour* around the construction and went on different roads to get to the zoo.

Provide an example of the word: You can ask students to elaborate on a word by giving an example of it.

1 **MR. MATHIS:** We have been reading about *tools*. Tools are something we hold in our hands that help us to do something. There are many kinds of tools we can use to help us. What is an example of a *tool*?

2 **QUINTERIA:** A hammer.

3 **MR. MATHIS:** A hammer is a tool. What does it help us do?

4 **QUINTERIA:** I don't know.

5 **MR. MATHIS:** A hammer can help us to build something with wood and nails.

Combine the Recast and Extend Strategies

Let's revisit Mrs. Rodriguez's conversation about properties of matter with her first graders. She recasts and extends the students' responses to model formal language structures— and she does it in a way that doesn't detract from the topic. When Strive-for-Five conversations contain open-ended questions *and* language modeling, the child is more likely to participate, as well as develop vocabulary (Cabell et al., 2015; Girolametto & Weitzman, 2002).

Watch a teacher model formal language structures.

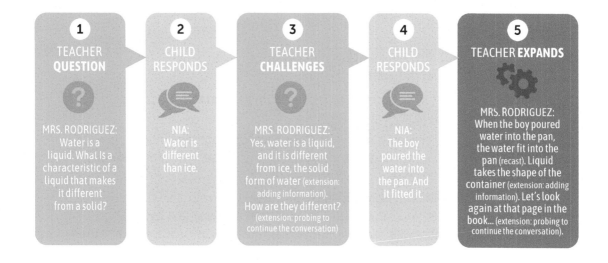

1
TEACHER QUESTION

MRS. RODRIGUEZ: Water is a liquid. What Is a characteristic of a liquid that makes it different from a solid?

2
CHILD RESPONDS

NIA: Water is different than ice.

3
TEACHER CHALLENGES

MRS. RODRIGUEZ: Yes, water is a liquid, and it is different from ice, the solid form of water (extension: adding information). How are they different? (extension: probing to continue the conversation)

4
CHILD RESPONDS

NIA: The boy poured the water into the pan. And it fitted it.

5
TEACHER EXPANDS

MRS. RODRIGUEZ: When the boy poured water into the pan, the water fit into the pan (recast). Liquid takes the shape of the container (extension: adding information). Let's look again at that page in the book... (extension: probing to continue the conversation).

Final Word: Close Strive-for-Five Conversations by Recasting and Extending

A lot of growth takes place in children's learning of language structures as children are developing. Conversations with preschoolers will feel very different from conversations with first graders. You can "tie a bow" at the end of every Strive-for-Five conversation by recasting and extending students' language to model formal language structures. We encourage you to keep conversations going, engaging young children in topics that interest them. Don't feel compelled to stop at five turns! Modeling lays a foundation for children's reading development.

> ### *Reflect and Implement*
>
> - Why is it important to model formal language structures for students?
> - Think of ways that your students are using conventional grammar (e.g., winned, goed, choosed) and consider how you can recast their words during conversation.
> - Think of a recent conversation you had with a student. How could you have extended what the student said by adding additional information or explanation or by prompting another conversation turn?

TAKING CONVERSATIONS BEYOND THE CLASSROOM

PART III

CHAPTER 9

Talking Is Teaching...

Strive-for-Five Conversations at Home

Imagine a parent and young child driving by a favorite grocery store and having this conversation:

1 DAD: Remember when we went there to get special foods for that big barbecue?

2 CHILD: Yeah, the party with grandma and the neighbors.

3 DAD: Right. I was thinking we could see if the neighbors want to do that again when the weather warms up. Would you like that?

4 CHILD: Yes! We goed there and got the goat.

5 DAD: That's right. We went to the grocery store and wanted to get a special kind of goat for the party.

This parent addresses past and future events that require abstract reasoning on the child's part, which is key to reading success, as discussed in Chapter 6. The child is eager to keep the conversation going, considering it doesn't stop at turn 4, after the parent asks a closed question (*Would you like that?*). When the child said "We goed" in turn 4, Dad repeated the phrase using conventional grammar.

Your students are already having conversations at home. You can enhance those conversations by partnering with and empowering parents and other family members to strive for five conversation turns. *Family-school partnerships* build cooperation, collaboration, and open communication between teachers and parents. When students have Strive-for-Five conversations at home, they complement the conversations you are having with them at school and further boost their language comprehension. This chapter provides suggestions for helping parents and family members understand that conversations matter for extending learning at home. Before jumping in, we offer a few assumptions underlying this chapter:

- Parents are children's first and most important teachers.
- All parents want their children to succeed in school and life.
- Families' unique cultures and structures influence how they support their children.

These assumptions, we hope, will help you develop positive, respectful relationships with parents and family members, which are necessary to partner with them in ways that support children's language and literacy skills. Of course, this chapter focuses on only one research-based home-school partnership goal of promoting children's language comprehension.

Resources for Family-School Partnerships

If you are looking for more comprehensive resources on family-school partnerships, check these out.

- Teachers can gain confidence and mindsets to create positive, empowering partnerships using the guidance in *Partnering with Families for Student Success: 24 Scenarios for Problem Solving with Parents* by Patricia A. Edwards and colleagues.
- Teachers and administrators can learn how to build meaningful partnerships with parents from Karen L. Mapp and colleagues' books and associated events, such as *Everyone Wins! : The Evidence for Family-School Partnerships & Implications for Practice.*
- *Family-School Partnerships During the Early School Years: Advancing Science to Influence Practice* by Karen L. Bierman and Susan M. Sheridan summarizes recent research on family engagement with implications for educators.

Encouraging Strive-for-Five Conversations at Home

When parents have Strive-for-Five conversations with their child, they involve themselves in their child's learning in a simple, yet effective way. Parents may be motivated to get involved in their child's learning in preschool and kindergarten, making these important times to capitalize on opportunities to engage families (Sheridan et al., 2020). The overarching term *parent involvement* includes what families do to support their child's learning at home or at school. There are two common types of parent involvement:

> **Home-based,** which may include parent-child conversations, reading together, and other informal learning experiences.

> **School-based,** which may include attending curriculum nights and parent-teacher conferences, volunteering in the classroom, and other school-based activities.

Strive-for-Five is all about home-based involvement in learning. Keep in mind that home-based parent involvement is often less visible because you will not have much evidence that shows whether parents have interacted with their child, but it is no less important than school-based parent involvement. Promoting home-based parent involvement in meaningful conversations can be an inclusive way to invite parents from diverse backgrounds to talk to their children about their family's values, culture, strengths, and funds of knowledge (McWayne et al., 2018).

Terms to Know

Family-School Partnerships is an approach to family engagement that emphasizes cooperation, collaboration, and open communication between teachers and parents and other caregivers in a child's life.

Home-Based Parent Involvement includes learning activities that happen at home, such as conversations and reading together.

Parent Involvement relates to what families do to support their child's learning at home and/or at school.

School-Based Parent Involvement includes communication efforts that happen at school, such as parent-teacher conferences, curriculum nights, and classroom volunteerism.

Evidence That Home Conversations Count!

Strive-for-Five conversations should happen at home because dialogue between parents and children is linked to later language skills (Anderson et al., 2021). The quality of the conversations and quantity of words children are exposed to at home matter. Quantity of words is especially important for toddlers, whereas quality of the conversations is especially important for preschoolers and older children, when they are learning to use more complex language (Anderson et al., 2021; Rowe, 2012). When teachers and parents have meaningful conversations with young children, it not only improves language skills, but also social and behavioral skills (Landry et al., 2017, Bierman et al., 2015). Young children develop larger vocabularies and are more engaged in book reading, compared to children who have conversations only at home or at school (Zucker et al., 2023).

So explain to parents that the simple act of having conversations with their children is actually teaching them so much! Here's what they gain, according to a comprehensive review by Haring Biel et al. (2020):

- Knowledge of their family and world
- Vocabulary they encounter during daily routines
- Models of mature language in their families' home language and dialect
- Trust that caring adults will guide them and offer feedback

Talking *is* teaching, and Strive-for-Five conversations are a great way to support learning at home (Zucker et al., 2021). In the next sections, we dig into specific ways you can empower parents to engage their children in Strive-for-Five conversations at home.

Promoting Strive-for-Five Conversations at Family Events

Family events, such as back-to-school night and a literacy or STEM fair, improve student learning when you give participants opportunities to practice what you're promoting, along with encouragement, support, and feedback (Grindal et al., 2016). With that in mind, at your next family event, you can follow these steps to engage families in Strive-for-Five conversations.

Step 1: Explain That Talking Is Teaching

The idea that "talking is teaching" may not be familiar to all parents. So it's helpful to explain that asking their children open-ended questions and engaging them in conversations benefits their children's learning—particularly, their language development and social-emotional development (Bierman et al., 2015; Garner et al., 2008; Haring Biel et al., 2020). In short, by explaining "talking is teaching," you provide parents with a rationale for Strive-for-Five conversations.

Step 2: Set the Stage for Success by Unplugging and Tuning In

Minimizing distractions from all types of screens—phones, laptops, TVs, tablets—is important if parents and children are going to have meaningful conversations. There is no way to unplug completely in most modern households (McDaniel, 2019). But you can encourage parents to set realistic goals, such as 5 to 15 minutes of undistracted conversation with their child each day. Urge them to determine a time and place to do that, and try to stick to it. If they have more than one child, ask them to plan family conversations, as well as individual conversations. The key message to parents is that they need to listen to their child during Strive-for-Five conversations by showing genuine interest in what their child is saying.

Step 3: Model Strive-for-Five Conversations

When you explain Strive-for-Five conversations to families, begin by defining just what those conversations are—a conversation between an adult and child that has at least five turns and is fueled by the child's observations and responses (Zucker et al., 2021). From there, screen short videos of real parents and children having conversations during play and family routines.

Another option is to model a conversation between you and a child, or another adult acting as a child, while parents use their fingers to count the turns in the conversation. As you model, note two hallmarks of Strive-for-Five conversations:

1. They usually start with an open-ended question. Explain that open-ended questions often start with a *wh* word (i.e., *where, when, why, who*) and require the child to use more than one word in his or her answer.

2. They build on what the child says or elaborates on his or her ideas. That is accomplished by asking follow-up questions, modeling mature grammar, or helping the child to think more deeply about the topic.

If time permits, explain how to avoid common "conversation stoppers" such as giving too little response time, using simple praise ("Good." "Nice."), or directing conversation away from the child's idea. Avoid educational terminology such as scaffolding or recasting. Instead, simply focus on the main goal of the conversation—to guide their children's learning by showing interest in their ideas.

Step 4: Provide Practice Opportunities With Support

To become comfortable in engaging in Strive-for-Five conversations, parents and children need opportunities to practice them. You might want to give a short, interactive read-aloud that includes stopping points for parents and children to turn and talk about ideas and questions the book inspires. You can set up activities around the room that promote conversations such as a wordless book station, and family drawing and storytelling. You may consider games inspired by products such as Scholastic's *Sticky Situation Cards*. As parents and children practice having conversations, circulate the room and point out these and other strategies you see parents using to keep conversations going.

Active Listening: Show genuine interest in what your child is saying.

Open-Ended Questions: Ask questions that encourage your child to think about and provide detailed responses.

Extend and Elaborate: Keep conversations going by expanding on your child's ideas and asking follow-up questions using mature grammar.

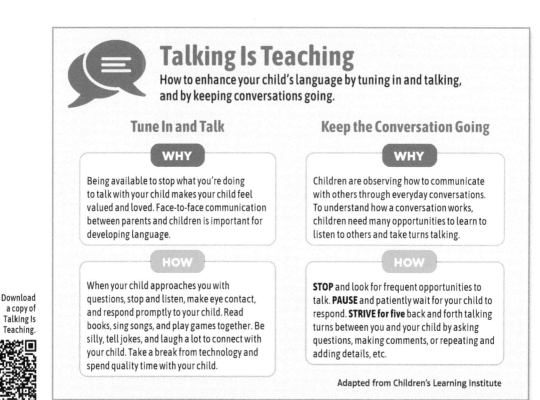

Download a copy of Talking Is Teaching.

Family handout to promote Strive-for-Five conversations at home

Consider creating a handout or email of strategies to help parents recall them when they're having conversations with their children at home.

PreK Family Engagement "Funshop" Event

Ms. Lester and Ms. Silva, PreK teachers at Thompson Elementary School in Spring, Texas, recently held an event that they advertised as a family "funshop" rather than a "workshop." At this one-hour event, they followed the four steps described above to empower families to infuse their existing routines with conversation. Ms. Lester, pictured in a bright yellow shirt in the photos below, told families, "You can strive for five or more conversation turns when you are in the kitchen, sharing a meal, or at bedtime" and "Families often have great Strive-for-Five conversations when they are on the go. For example, the car is a great time for you to strike up a conversation with your child." She invited families to watch as she modeled strategies during a short, interactive read-aloud.

During the second half of the funshop event, Ms. Lester and Ms. Silva organized activity stations around the room for parents to practice having conversations with their children. Each station had bilingual instructions available. The teachers circulated the room to provide encouragement and feedback, as you can see Ms. Lester providing to a mom and daughter in the photo below, as they did an activity called "Story Bags." Ms. Lester said, "I noticed you're having fun making up a story to go with the items in your bag. Mom, you're doing a great job of asking open-ended questions and making eye contact to show Mayra that you're enjoying her story."

Story Bags

TALKING IS TEACHING

You and your child will create a story in a bag.

Materials needed:
- Assorted foam shapes
- Snack size zipper bag
- Hair gel
- Baby wipes
- Clear packing tape
- Table liner

1. **Choose 3–5 items** to create your own story. Put them in your bag.

2. Add **2–3 squirts** of gel into your bag and **seal it closed** with packing tape.

3. Tell your child a story first. Say, **"I can make up a story with the things in my bag."**
   - I picked this because it represents...
   - This reminds me of...
   - Once upon a time...

4. **Have your child tell you his/her story.** Make comments or ask questions about his/her story.
   Questions to ask:
   - What does this mean to you?
   - What's happening in your story?
   - Tell me more.

Family engagement activity stations with teacher support

Download a copy of "Story Bags."

Aligning School-Home Conversations

For decades, parents have been asking their children the same question every day: "What did you learn at school today?" And for decades, they've been getting the same response: "Nothing." Strive-for-Five conversations can bring that to an end as parents learn how to start meaningful conversations. Here are three contexts that support meaningful conversations at home.

During Book Reading

When parents read and talk about books with their children, it promotes language and literacy development (Dowdall et al., 2020). So we encourage you to encourage family reading! Children should take an active role in talking about books, rather than passively listening (Pillinger et al., 2022). Parents can accomplish that by asking open-ended questions while they're reading. Give them examples of concrete questions and abstract questions they might ask their child, such as, "What's happening here?" or "What are you curious about on this page?" Encourage parents to pause frequently to discuss interesting facts, events, characters' thinking, and illustrations. You can help families create shared book reading routines that fit their family

Use Acronyms to Help Parents Talk With Their Kids

Many educators use catchy acronyms to help parents have conversations with their children. Consider sharing the ones below.

The PEER acronym for how to support conversations during book reading (Arnold et al., 1994; Pillinger et al., 2022) is especially well suited for parents of preschoolers.

- **P:** Prompt the child to name objects in illustrations or talk about characters and events in the book.
- **E:** Evaluate if the child is correct. If not, add details and teach new vocabulary.
- **E:** Expand on the child's response by restating it with a bit more detail.
- **R:** Repeat the conversation cycle or ask the child to repeat a sentence you modeled.

The READY acronym (Rowe et al., 2023) helps parents engage their children in conversations about abstract topics such as special family memories or future plans.

- **R:** Recall past events.
- **E:** Explain new words and concepts.
- **A:** Ask lots of questions.
- **D:** Discuss the future.
- **Y:** You can make a difference in your child's academic success when you talk together.

schedule. Explain how families often read books in the evening or as part of bedtime rituals to promote a lifelong love of reading (Strommen & Mates, 2004). Additionally, encourage parents of multilingual learners to read aloud in their home language because it supports development of that language and English (Roberts, 2008).

Culture and Languages
Social Values
Economy

Local Government
Media
Community Resource

School
Home

Child

During Meals and Meal Preparation

Encourage parents to embed conversations into routines such as snack and meal times to support their child's language (Rowe et al., 2023; Suskind et al., 2015). During meals, parents can talk about past and future events and how to make healthy eating decisions (Leech et al., 2018; Sharma et al., 2011). Meal prep and cooking are also excellent times to talk with young children as you get them involved in measuring, peeling, chopping, or other kitchen activities.

During Play

Families can have meaningful conversations that build children's vocabulary and language by explaining or elaborating on what they are doing during play (Heidlage et al., 2020; Rowe et al., 2023). You can help families create Strive-for-Five opportunities during these routines by reminding parents that they should follow their child's interest while also explaining new words and concepts (Landry et al., 2017). Busy families can integrate simple play activities even when they are on the go. For example, parents may keep a few small toys in their car to pass time when waiting for a sibling's event. Other parents find ways to explore nature on walks to/from school or by noticing interesting things during their drive home.

Giving Parents Conversation Starters

Offer parents ideas for starting Strive-for-Five conversations, such as placing paper "chat bands" around children's wrists or "Ask me about..." stickers on their shirts as they leave to go home.

You might send text messages on a regular basis to nudge parents in the right direction (Castleman, 2015). We use text messages to promote conversations at home (Cabell et al., 2019; Zucker et al., 2021). We recommend sending them up to three times a week and including parent-friendly tips and information (York et al., 2019). See a sample schedule on the next page. To make your effort even more effective, consider personalizing your messages to address the needs, desires, and interests of individual students (Doss et al., 2019).

Supporting Culturally and Linguistically Diverse Families

The number of multilingual learners and students from diverse cultural backgrounds is increasing in the United States (Silverman et al., 2014). Family engagement efforts that are responsive to families' home languages and cultures benefit children's learning (Larson et al., 2020). As you encourage families to engage in Strive-for-Five conversations, capitalize on their unique, existing home cultures. Here are some conversation starters that have worked well for us to help families talk about their stories and values:

- **Family stories:** "Did you know that one time...?" (Share a special family experience or a story from your childhood.)
- **Silly ideas:** "If you were a holiday, what would you be?" (Talk about holidays or traditions your family celebrates.)
- **Tall tales:** "I will tell you an unusual 'story' from our family. Can you guess whether it is true or make-believe?" (Make this game a fun way for your child to guess if a story is real or silly while also sharing important information about unique family stories or values.)

Parent Text Message Examples to Promote Strive-for-Five Conversations at Home

Week	Monday Messages	Wednesday Messages	Friday Messages
1	Thanks for joining this text messaging program from your child's school. You'll receive texts three times a week. These texts will help you get ready for kindergarten. They will include tips and simple activities that promote learning and communication.	We will be sending ideas to spark conversations with your child every week. When kids take turns in conversations they build important language skills! Avoid asking general questions like, "How was your day?" Instead, talk about specific subjects at school, or ask about what they ate, or the games they played.	Let's practice asking specific questions with this activity! Using pictures, ask your child to identify his or her favorite things. Once you have a couple pictures of their favorite things, glue them on to 1–2 pages in their learning journals! See the link for details: **My Favorite Things** cliengagefamily.org/my-favorite-things/
2	Let's keep the conversations going! Set aside 15 minutes to read, talk, sing, or play with your child. Ask him or her, "What do you want to play together?"	Self-control and cooperation are important for success in school. You can help your child develop these skills by talking about different behaviors. Ask your child, "How would we act at a circus? What about at the supermarket? And at the library?" Take turns acting it out, too!	Let's keep building cooperation skills. Try playing the "Quiet & Loud" game! Distinguish between using quiet, medium, and loud voices. See the link below: **Quiet and Loud** cliengagefamily.org/quiet-and-loud/
3	New week, new conversations! Turn-taking is a great skill to get us ready for school! Aim for four to five turns in conversations with your child today! Try describing different feelings to your child. Take turns talking about things that make you happy, sad, mad, scared, and excited.	Honest conversations about feelings builds trust. Today, let's talk about things that make us happy. Ask your child, "What made you happy today? Why?" Make sure to ask about hard parts of your child's day and don't be afraid to share something good and challenging from your day, too.	Tell a story about something that happened last week. Say, "Remember when…" and ask, "How did you feel?" Incorporate these conversations into this week's "Picture Placemats" activity! See link for details: **Picture Placemats** cliengagefamily.org/picture-placemats/
4	We hope you're having meaningful conversations and interactions with your child as you explore these activities and tips. Don't forget, kids need time to think about how to answer questions. While talking with your child this week, remember to wait for him or her to respond.	Talking about what your child is doing can help him or her learn important vocabulary words. If your child is playing with toys, say, "You are stacking your blocks into a high tower. How high do you think it can go?"	Learning how to communicate and use language are important skills. Here, your child will use descriptive language to describe familiar pictures. Remember to ask open-ended questions! See the link for details: **Roll and Tell** cliengagefamily.org/roll-and-tell/

Other ways to show respect for the diverse families you serve is to provide home-school communications in the family's preferred language. You can use online translation tools to provide conversation starters in multiple languages. If possible, ask colleagues or parents who speak those languages to review your conversation starters for accuracy.

Empower families that speak a language other than English to keep speaking their home language especially as children transition to school. Parents may hold misconceptions about multilingual language development or worry that their child will be confused by trying to learn two or more languages. For example, some parents think they should focus only on English because it is dominant in U.S. schools. Educators can dispel these myths. Remind parents there are many benefits to being bilingual, including (Blanc et al., 2022; Van den Noort et al., 2019):

> **Cultural Benefits:** When children are fluent in their home language, they can share stories and communicate with other family members and across generations. Being bilingual can also promote sensitivity across cultures.

> **Economic Benefits:** Bilinguals often have a competitive advantage in the marketplace. In many industries, you can earn a higher salary if you are able to speak and translate languages.

Recognize Families' Cultural Background and Socializing Styles

A family's cultural background and socializing style influence how parents communicate with their children (Rogoff et al., 2015). This also influences how parents and children talk and explore early literacy (Serpell et al., 2002). For example, children from indigenous cultures across the world and Hispanic/Latine cultures are often socialized to complete household tasks collaboratively, whereas American, middle-class children of European descent are often socialized to complete tasks independently (Coppens & Rogoff, 2022; López et al., 2012). Some children's cultural backgrounds may promote more collaborative learning whereas children in other family cultures may be encouraged to work more independently (Correa-Chávez et al., 2016; Dayton et al., 2022).

These findings suggest that we should not assume our students' parents share our beliefs about how to raise children effectively and support their learning. All families value their children's learning, but may take different pathways to support that learning, especially during their early years of school (Simons et al., 2021).

Cognitive Benefits: Bilinguals routinely switch between languages, which is also an indicator of strong executive function, which is a set of skills that allow us to have self-control, follow directions, and set goals. They may have an advantage with problem-solving tasks because these skills are used in communication across languages and cultures.

So encourage parents to talk and read to their children in their home language.

As you engage with families, keep in mind that all families want to support their children's learning, regardless of their culture or background. But the ways they provide that support may differ across cultures and backgrounds. For more information, see the box on page 140.

Final Word: Empower Families to Strive for Five

Strive-for-Five conversations at home are a low-cost, effective way to involve families in their children's learning. It is important to help families see the important role they play in extending learning by talking to their children in ways that prompt talk about the past, present, and future, and their family's unique stories. "Unplugging and tuning into" their children's messages is a habit that will benefit their children throughout their school years. Language and literacy skills soar when children are supported at school and home by responsive conversation partners.

Reflect and Implement

In what ways do you and/or your colleagues encourage parent involvement? Within that structure, is there a space for you to discuss with parents the importance of conversations at home?

Fostering parent involvement is similar to fostering any relationship. It takes time to build willingness and trust. What is one idea that you can take away from this chapter that you can approach parents with this month?

Consider the family makeup of your students. What resources or materials might they find helpful?

In what ways are you supporting culturally and linguistically diverse families in your classroom? What can you take away from this chapter to support engagement in Strive-for-Five conversations at home?

CHAPTER 10

Take the...

Strive-for-Five Conversation Challenge!

We hope you are excited to have more Strive-for-Five conversations with your students. When you do, you will accelerate their language comprehension and literacy by stretching a typical conversation into at least five turns. Teachers who stretch conversations:

- Actively listen to what children say and respond by following their lead.

- Ask open-ended questions about concrete and abstract ideas to spark meaningful conversations.

- Use scaffolding strategies to simplify the conversation or make it more challenging, depending on the children's response.

We challenge you to start by adding Strive-for-Five conversations to one of your daily classroom routines. When you've mastered that, add it to another part of your day. When teachers in Texas challenged themselves to engage their students in Strive-for-Five conversations, here is what they had to say:

> "With the Strive-for-Five framework, I go way deeper than I used to. I'm asking far more higher order thinking questions, and my kids, they get it! Then, I'm like 'Oh my! You're ready for this!'"

> "I appreciate the scaffolding strategies because I was used to scaffolding up, but not down. Now I have tools to do both, and it's very helpful, especially with my students with limited English."

> "This method facilitates higher-level thinking responses from my PreK students... I've noticed that the students anticipate me stopping in read-alouds to ask them questions. They have gotten better at speaking in full sentences and applying what they've learned in drawings, through play, and at recess."

In this final chapter, we review the reasons for taking time to engage your students in Strive-for-Five in conversations. Then we provide tools to make those conversations part of your routine and reflect on ways to improve on them.

A Recap of How Little Kids Grow With Big Conversations

The goal of the Strive-for-Five framework is to support language comprehension and literacy in preschool to first-grade students. Abundant research finds multiple benefits of extending conversations with young children (Bierman et al., 2015; Cabell et al., 2015; Hadley et al., 2019; Landry et al., 2017; Rowe et al., 2023; Wasik & Hindman, 2011a and 2011b; Zucker et al., 2021, 2023):

1. You build trust and a strong teacher-student or parent-child relationship when you take time to connect via conversations.

2. You elevate the quality of discourse in your classroom and family's homes when you focus on stretching conversations.

3. You increase children's language comprehension and conversation skills when Strive-for-Five conversations are part of children's routines.

Here are ways to use Strive-for-Five conversations to support the language comprehension strands of Scarborough's Reading Rope:

Literacy knowledge Read aloud narrative and informational genres and explain features of diverse types of texts.

Vocabulary Build broad and deep vocabulary by explicitly teaching sets of related words and encouraging students to use advanced vocabulary in conversations.

Verbal reasoning Ask questions that require increasingly complex, abstract reasoning in a variety of classroom contexts.

Background knowledge Immerse students in conversations about content areas to build knowledge during read-alouds, play, science explorations, and social studies units.

Language structures Recast and extend students' messages to model mature syntax and grammar during conversations.

These early language and literacy skills ensure later reading comprehension (Castles et al., 2018).

Building Chat Habits

Teachers who embrace the Strive-for-Five framework adopt the "conversations count" mindset. That means they slow down to listen to children and respond in ways that keep conversations going. At first, that may seem to require a lot of effort and in-the-moment decision-making (Borko et al., 2008), but over time you will identify the moments that lend themselves to Strive-for-Five conversations. Teachers tell us that once they have adopted a "conversations count" mindset, they find it easier to engage in Strive-for-Five conversations with students and elicit more information from them.

Teachers often ask us how to establish routines that allow for Strive-for-Five conversations beyond the suggestions we've made thus far, such as interactive read-alouds and knowledge-building approaches. We recommend you start by picking a routine, such as read-aloud or outdoor play, and challenge yourself to have at least three Strive-for-Five conversations during that routine. The next step is to have a daily Strive-for-Five conversation with

MONTHLY HABIT TRACKER

WORK HABITS	WEEK 1					WEEK 2					WEEK 3					WEEK 4					TOTAL
	1	2	3	4	5	1	2	3	4	5	1	2	3	4	5	1	2	3	4	5	
Have 3 Conversations During Read-Aloud.	✔		✔		✔			✔		✔	✔		✔		✔	✔	✔	✔	✔		12
Use Equity Sticks During Read-Aloud.	✔		✔		✔			✔		✔	✔		✔		✔	✔	✔	✔	✔		12
Teach 2 Words With Vocabulary Picture Cards.	✔		✔		✔			✔		✔	✔		✔			✔		✔			9
Text Conversation Starters to Families.					✔					✔	✔				✔	✔					5

Download the "Monthly Habit Tracker."

each student using equity sticks. When you've taken that step, you might move to integrating Strive-for-Five conversations into a larger "habit tracker" such as the one shown.

You may have some students who would benefit from more Strive-for-Five conversations, such as your multilingual learners. To help teachers identify those students and use their time wisely, our coaches have encouraged them to use a "Chat Planner" to select students with limited language at the beginning of the year or who show limited language skills at progress-monitoring times in the middle of the year. Set specific conversation goals for these students to prioritize. You can see in the example on the next page, the planner allows teachers to focus on topics or skills that will support selected students most. Teachers often choose multilingual learners for small-group or one-on-one conversations to ensure they develop English proficiency (Gersten et al., 2007).

In addition to making plans for supporting students with limited language skills, take note of students with advanced language skills who can help you model conversations, as you teach new routines such using equity sticks and turn and talk, which we explained in Chapter 3. When you see students being good conversationalists, praise them along these lines: "I noticed you were listening and nodding during that turn and talk," or "You asked your partner questions

WEEKLY CHAT PLANNER

WEEK OF:

Kids to Chat With	Chat Topic	Chat Complete?
Name: Raphael	☑ Knowledge building ☑ Vocabulary ☐ Abstract thinking ☐ Social skills, problem-solving ☐ Emotion naming	☑ Yes with upward scaffold ☐ Yes with downward scaffold ☐ No
Name: Katja	☑ Knowledge building ☐ Vocabulary ☐ Abstract thinking ☑ Social skills, problem-solving ☐ Emotion naming	☐ Yes with upward scaffold ☐ Yes with downward scaffold ☑ No
Name: Simon	☐ Knowledge building ☐ Vocabulary ☐ Abstract thinking ☐ Social skills, problem-solving ☑ Emotion naming	☐ Yes with upward scaffold ☑ Yes with downward scaffold ☐ No
Name: Jo	☐ Knowledge building ☑ Vocabulary ☐ Abstract thinking ☐ Social skills, problem-solving ☐ Emotion naming	☑ Yes with upward scaffold ☐ Yes with downward scaffold ☐ No
Name: Chester	☑ Knowledge building ☑ Vocabulary ☐ Abstract thinking ☐ Social skills, problem-solving ☐ Emotion naming	☐ Yes with upward scaffold ☑ Yes with downward scaffold ☐ No
Name: Savannah	☐ Knowledge building ☑ Vocabulary ☐ Abstract thinking ☐ Social skills, problem-solving ☐ Emotion naming	☐ Yes with upward scaffold ☐ Yes with downward scaffold ☑ No

Download the "Weekly Chat Planner."

that showed you wanted to learn more about their ideas." This creates a positive culture and takes full responsibility of modeling conversations off you and shares it with other strong language users in the classroom.

Setting Instructional Goals by Reflecting on Your Conversation Style

Return to this question from Chapter 1: Who are the people in your life that you most enjoy talking with? Are there ways they extend meaningful conversations that you want to bring to your Strive-for-Five approach? In many ways, becoming a good conversationalist is an art form without a single approach. The Strive-for-Five framework helps teachers to think strategically about how to scaffold learning and model mature language.

Next, think about times in the day when you can most easily strike up conversations. As you know, the classroom has certain times of the day that lend themselves to deeper conversations, such as read-alouds and small-group time. But intentional conversations can happen in formal and informal learning contexts. Consider how you can set goals to add more Strive-for-Five conversations in these settings over time.

Formal situations include:

- Interactive read-alouds
- Circle time or whole-group time
- Small-group time
- Individual play or work at centers, workstations, etc.

Informal situations include:

- Meal or snack times
- Transition times (e.g., arrival/dismissal, handwashing)
- Outdoor play or recess

Striving for Five With a Trusted Colleague

Consider taking the Strive-for-Five challenge with a trusted colleague. It may be easier to slow down and reflect on your conversation mindset and decisions with a partner than trying to do it on your own. You may even want to videotape yourselves interacting with children in your classrooms (Zucker et al., 2020, 2021). Playing back and reflecting on the videos with your colleague and/or, perhaps, instructional coach is a good way to "debrief" on conversations and think about the decisions you're making (Wasik & Hindman, 2011a and 2011b; Elek & Page, 2019). Here's a summary of what Ms. Guiron, a kindergarten teacher, and her coach learned across a series of video reflection sessions focused on Strive-for-Five conversations (Zucker et al., 2021).

SESSION 1: Ms. Guiron felt that it was "hard to process it all because it is valuable, but is overwhelming" to think of the time and skills needed to scaffold the countless conversations that occur during a school day. Her coach agreed and advised her to avoid striving for five turns in every conversation, and instead start only during whole-group book reading. So, they captured a video of Ms. Guiron reading aloud the informational book *The Way I Feel* by Janan Cain.

SESSION 2: They played back the video and counted the number of turns Ms. Guiron had with the children during conversations. They paused the video often to slow down the flurry of classroom activity. That is when Ms. Guiron noticed, "When I asked a question and a child responded correctly, I moved on. And if a child answered incorrectly, I moved to another child." I allowed just two or three conversation turns for most students. She and her coach discussed why and decided it was because she felt spending too much time talking during read-alouds might lead to students misbehaving. But Ms. Guiron agreed to try a bit more scaffolding and skipping pages if she noticed students getting antsy. She and her coach set a goal for her to have a Strive-for-Five conversation with three children during a specific time of day—*after* whole-group book reading.

SESSION 3: This time they played back a read-aloud of *My BIG Feelings: In Five Small Tales* by Sidney Hall. It was then that Ms. Guiron realized, "I have the heart for this" because she saw that when she stuck with one student for a few more turns and kept the conversation going, it positively affected *all* her students. Even when the student answered incorrectly, she could see him relax as she scaffolded downward so that he could give a meaningful response. Students who answered correctly enjoyed the feedback loop because it enabled them to build knowledge on top of the knowledge they had.

We know there are many factors that influence your decisions during lessons. You also make hundreds of instructional decisions each day! Sometimes you will make a logical decision to keep a conversation short and sweet, due to time constraints or other factors. You don't have to make every conversation perfect. Start reflecting on your use of questions and language facilitation strategies and set goals with a coach or trusted colleague to support your students' language comprehension (Domitrovich et al., 2009; Landry et al., 2017, 2021).

Final Word: Take the Strive-for-Five Conversation Challenge

We encourage you to challenge yourself to have more Strive-for-Five conversations with your students—more meaningful and extended conversations. As you do that, be gracious to yourself. Your conversations don't need to be perfect for students to benefit from them and build language comprehension skills they need for later reading. The first step may be changing your mindset on talk, its importance, and how talking with children adds up over time. This should not be a hard sell because we are confident that your kids can help you enjoy the rest of the conversation, as young children are fascinating to talk to! So reflect on your conversations each day not only to determine what is and isn't working instructionally, but also to enjoy the wonderful things your students say.

Reflect and Implement

What are your three biggest takeaways from this book about Strive-for-Five conversations?

Who were the good conversationalists in your childhood that you want to echo with your students?

Where can you see evidence of a "conversations count" mindset making a difference for your students or in your own personal life?

If habit trackers are something that might support you, which kind would be most useful for you? Why?

Record a short video of your classroom conversations (e.g., five minutes or less). Reflect on your own or with a colleague. What went well? What might you change? At what points in the school day would you like to focus on to improve your Strive-for-Five conversations? Why?

Cummins, J. (2017). Teaching for transfer in multilingual school contexts. *Bilingual and Multilingual Education*, 103–115.

Cunningham, A. E., & Stanovich, K. E. (1991). Tracking the unique effects of print exposure in children: Associations with vocabulary, general knowledge, and spelling. *Journal of Educational Psychology*, 83(2), 264–274.

Cunningham, A. E., & Stanovich, K. E. (1998). What reading does for the mind. *American Educator*, 22, 8–17.

Dayton, A., Aceves-Azuara, I., & Rogoff, B. (2022). Collaboration at a microscale: Cultural differences in family interactions. *British Journal of Developmental Psychology*, 40(2), 189–213.

Deshmukh, R. S., Pentimonti, J. M., Zucker, T. A., & Curry, B. (2022). Teachers' use of scaffolds within conversations during shared book reading. *Language, Speech, and Hearing Services in Schools*, 53(1), 150–166.

Deshmukh, R. S., Zucker, T. A., Tambyraja, S. R., Pentimonti, J. M., Bowles, R. P., & Justice, L. M. (2019). Teachers' use of questions during shared book reading: Relations to child responses. *Early Childhood Research Quarterly*, 49, 59–68.

Dickinson, D. K. (2003). Why we must improve teacher-child conversations in preschools and the promise of professional development. In L. Girolametto and E. Weitzman (Eds.), *Enhancing caregiver language facilitation in childcare settings*. The Hanen Institute.

Dickinson, D. K., & Porche, M. V. (2011). Relation between language experiences in preschool classrooms and children's kindergarten and fourth-grade language and reading abilities. *Child Development*, 82(3), 870–886.

Dickinson, D. K., & Smith, M. W. (1994). Long-term effects of preschool teachers' book readings on low-income children's vocabulary and story comprehension. *Reading Research Quarterly*, 29(2), 104.

Dickinson, D. K., Nesbitt, K. T., Collins, M. F., Hadley, E. B., Newman, K., Rivera, B. L., Ilgez, H., Nicolopoulou, A., Golinkoff, R. M., & Hirsh-Pasek, K. (2019). Teaching for breadth and depth of vocabulary knowledge: Learning from explicit and implicit instruction and the storybook texts. *Early Childhood Research Quarterly*, 47, 341–356.

Diprossimo, L., Ushakova, A., Zoski, J., Gamble, H., Irey, R., & Cain, K. (2023). The associations between child and item characteristics, use of vocabulary scaffolds, and reading comprehension in a digital environment: Insights from a big data approach. *Contemporary Educational Psychology*, 73, 102165.

Domitrovich, C. E., Gest, S. D., Gill, S., Bierman, K. L., Welsh, J. A., & Jones, D. (2009). Fostering high-quality teaching with an enriched curriculum and professional development support: The Head Start REDI program. *American Educational Research Journal*, 46(2), 567–597.

Donovan, C. A., & Smolkin, L. B. (2001). Genre and other factors influencing teachers' book selections for science instruction. *Reading Research Quarterly*, 36(4), 412–440.

Donovan, C. A., & Smolkin, L. B. (2002). Considering genre, content, and visual features in the selection of trade books for science instruction. *The Reading Teacher*, 55(6), 502–520.

Doss, C., Fahle, E. M., Loeb, S., & York, B. N. (2019). More than just a nudge. *Journal of Human Resources*, 54(3), 567–603.

Dowdall, N., Melendez-Torres, G. J., Murray, L., Gardner, F., Hartford, L., & Cooper, P. J. (2020). Shared picture book reading interventions for child language development: A systematic review and meta-analysis. *Child Development*, 91(2), e383–e399.

Duke, N. K., & Bennett-Armistead, V. S. (2003). *Reading & writing informational text in the primary grades*. Scholastic Teaching Resources.

Duke, N. K., & Carlisle, J. (2011). The development of comprehension. In M. L. Kamil, P. D. Pearson, E. Birr Moje, & P. P. Afflerbach (Eds.), *Handbook of reading research* (Volume IV, pp. 199–228). Routledge.

Duke, N. K., & Cartwright, K. B. (2021). The science of reading progresses: Communicating advances beyond the simple view of reading. *Reading Research Quarterly*, 56(S1).

Duke, N. K., Ward, A. E., & Pearson, P. D. (2021). The science of reading comprehension instruction. *The Reading Teacher*, 74(6), 663–672.

Early, D. M., Iruka, I. U., Ritchie, S., Barbarin, O. A., Winn, D.-M. C., Crawford, G. M., Frome, P. M., Clifford, R. M., Burchinal, M., Howes, C., Bryant, D. M., & Pianta, R. C. (2010). How do pre-kindergarteners spend their time? Gender, ethnicity, and income as predictors of experiences in pre-kindergarten classrooms. *Early Childhood Research Quarterly*, 25(2), 177–193.

EdReports. (2022). *State of the instructional materials market 2021: The availability and use of aligned materials*. https://www.edreports.org/resources/article/state-of-the-instructional-materials-market-2021-the-availability-and-use-of-aligned-materials

Ehri, L. C. (2005). Learning to read words: Theory, findings, and issues. *Scientific Studies of Reading*, 9(2), 167–188.

Elek, C., & Page, J. (2019). Critical features of effective coaching for early childhood educators: A review of empirical research literature. *Professional Development in Education*, 45(4), 567–585.

Flood, J., Lapp, D., & Brice Heath, S. (2004). Bridging home and school literacies: Models for culturally responsive teaching, a case for African-American English. *Handbook of research on teaching literacy through the communicative and visual arts* (pp. 365–375). Routledge.

Foorman, B., Beyler, N., Borradaile, K., Coyne, M., Denton, C. A., Dimino, J., Hayes, L., Justice, L., Warnick, L., & Wagner, R. (2016). Foundational skills to support reading for understanding in kindergarten through 3rd grade. *Educator's Practice Guide*. NCEE 2016-4008. What Works Clearinghouse.

French, L. (2004). Science as the center of a coherent, integrated early childhood curriculum. *Early Childhood Research Quarterly*, 19(1), 138–149.

Fumero, K. (2022). Supportive language strategies for preschool dual-language learners: Associations to early language outcomes. Florida State University.

Garner, P. W., Dunsmore, J. C., & Southam-Gerrow, M. (2008). Mother–child conversations about emotions: Linkages to child aggression and prosocial behavior. *Social Development*, 17(2), 259–277.

Gaudreau, C., Bustamante, A. S., Hirsh-Pasek, K., & Golinkoff, R. M. (2021). Questions in a life-sized board game: Comparing caregivers' and children's question-asking across STEM museum exhibits. *Mind, Brain, and Education*, 15(2), 199–210.

Gersten, R., Baker, S. K., Shanahan, T., Linan-Thompson, S., Collins, P., & Scarcella, R. (2007). Effective literacy and English language instruction for English learners in the elementary grades. *IES Practice Guide*. NCEE 2007-4011. What Works Clearinghouse.

Gest, S. D., Holland-Coviello, R., Welsh, J. A., Eicher-Catt, D. L., & Gill, S. (2006). Language development subcontexts in Head Start classrooms: Distinctive patterns of teacher talk during free play, mealtime, and book reading. *Early Education and Development*, 17(2), 293–315.

Girolametto, L., & Weitzman, E. (2002). Responsiveness of child care providers in interactions with toddlers and preschoolers. *Language, Speech, and Hearing Services in Schools*, 33(4), 268–281.

Girolametto, L., Weitzman, E., van Lieshout, R., & Duff, D. (2000). Directiveness in teachers' language input to toddlers and preschoolers in day care. *Journal of Speech, Language, and Hearing Research*, 43(5), 1101–1114.

Goldenberg, C. (2013). Unlocking the research on English learners: What we know—and don't yet know—about effective instruction. *American Educator*, 37(2), 4.

Golinkoff, R. M., Hirsh-Pasek, K., & Singer, D. G. (2006). Why play = learning: A challenge for parents and educators. In D. G. Singer, R. M. Golinkoff, & K. Hirsh-Pasek (Eds.), *Play = learning: How play motivates and enhances children's cognitive and social-emotional growth*. Oxford University Press.

Gonzalez, J. E., Durán, L., Linan-Thompson, S., & Jimerson, S. R. (2022). Unlocking the promise of multitiered systems of support (MTSS) for linguistically diverse students: Advancing science, practice, and equity. *School Psychology Review*, 51(4), 387–391.

Gonzalez, J. E., Pollard-Durodola, S., Simmons, D. C., Taylor, A. B., Davis, M. J., Fogarty, M., & Simmons, L. (2014). Enhancing preschool children's vocabulary: Effects of teacher talk before, during and after shared reading. *Early Childhood Research Quarterly, 29*(2), 214–226.

Gonzalez, J. E., Pollard-Durodola, S., Simmons, D. C., Taylor, A. B., Davis, M. J., Kim, M., & Simmons, L. (2010). Developing low-income preschoolers' social studies and science vocabulary knowledge through content-focused shared book reading. *Journal of Research on Educational Effectiveness, 4*(1), 25–52.

Goodwin, A. P., Cho, S.-J., Reynolds, D., Silverman, R., & Nunn, S. (2021). Explorations of classroom talk and links to reading achievement in upper elementary classrooms. *Journal of Educational Psychology, 113*(1), 27–48.

Gough, P. B., & Tunmer, W. E. (1986). Decoding, reading, and reading disability. *Remedial and Special Education, 7*(1), 6–10.

Gray, S., & Brinkley, S. (2011). Fast mapping and word learning by preschoolers with specific language impairment in a supported learning context: Effect of encoding cues, phonotactic probability, and object familiarity. *Journal of Speech, Language, and Hearing Research, 54*(3), 870–884.

Greenfield, D. B., Jirout, J., Dominguez, X., Greenberg, A., Maier, M., & Fuccillo, J. (2009). Science in the preschool classroom: A programmatic research agenda to improve science readiness. *Early Education and Development, 20*(2), 238–264.

Grindal, T., Bowne, J. B., Yoshikawa, H., Schindler, H. S., Duncan, G. J., Magnuson, K., & Shonkoff, J. P. (2016). The added impact of parenting education in early childhood education programs: A meta-analysis. *Children and Youth Services Review, 70*, 238–249.

Grusec, J. E., & Davidov, M. (2021). *Socializing Children*. Cambridge University Press.

Guo, Y., Wang, S., Hall, A. H., Breit-Smith, A., & Busch, J. (2015). The effects of science instruction on young children's vocabulary learning: A research synthesis. *Early Childhood Education Journal, 44*(4), 359–367.

Hadley, E. B., Barnes, E. M., Wiernik, B. M., & Raghavan, M. (2022). A meta-analysis of teacher language practices in early childhood classrooms. *Early Childhood Research Quarterly, 59*, 186–202.

Hadley, E. B., Dickinson, D. K., Hirsh-Pasek, K., & Golinkoff, R. M. (2019). Building semantic networks: The impact of a vocabulary intervention on preschoolers' depth of word knowledge. *Reading Research Quarterly, 54*(1), 41–61.

Hadley, E. B., & Mendez, K. Z. (2021). A systematic review of word selection in early childhood vocabulary instruction. *Early Childhood Research Quarterly, 54*, 44–59.

Hadley, E. B., Newman, K. M., & Mock, J. (2020). Setting the stage for talk: Strategies for encouraging language-building conversations. *The Reading Teacher, 74*(1), 39–48.

Hamre, B. K., Justice, L. M., Pianta, R. C., Kilday, C., Sweeney, B., Downer, J. T., & Leach, A. (2010). Implementation fidelity of MyTeachingPartner literacy and language activities: Association with preschoolers' language and literacy growth. *Early Childhood Research Quarterly, 25*(3), 329–347.

Haring Biel, C., Buzhardt, J., Brown, J. A., Romano, M. K., Lorio, C. M., Windsor, K. S., Kaczmarek, L. A., Gwin, R., Sandall, S. S., & Goldstein, H. (2020). Language interventions taught to caregivers in homes and classrooms: A review of intervention and implementation fidelity. *Early Childhood Research Quarterly, 50*, 140–156.

Heidlage, J. K., Cunningham, J. E., Kaiser, A. P., Trivette, C. M., Barton, E. E., Frey, J. R., & Roberts, M. Y. (2020). The effects of parent-implemented language interventions on child linguistic outcomes: A meta-analysis. *Early Childhood Research Quarterly, 50*, 6–23.

Hendricks, A. E., Adlof, S. M., Alonzo, C. N., Fox, A. B., & Hogan, T. P. (2019). Identifying children at risk for developmental language disorder using a brief, whole-classroom screen. *Journal of Speech, Language, and Hearing Research, 62*(4), 896–908.

Henrichs, J., Rescorla, L., Schenk, J. J., Schmidt, H. G., Jaddoe, V. W., Hofman, A., Raat, H., Verhulst, F. C., & Tiemeier, H. (2011). Examining continuity of early expressive vocabulary development: The Generation R study. *Journal of Speech, Language, and Hearing Research, 54*(3), 854–869.

Hindman, A. H., Wasik, B. A., & Bradley, D. E. (2019). How classroom conversations unfold: Exploring teacher–child exchanges during shared book reading. *Early Education and Development, 30*(4), 478–495.

Hirsh-Pasek, K., Golinkoff, R. M., Berk, L. E., & Singer, D. G. (2008). *A mandate for playful learning in preschool: Presenting the evidence*. Oxford University Press.

Hjetland, H. N., Brinchmann, E. I., Scherer, R., Hulme, C., & Melby-Lervåg, M. (2020). Preschool pathways to reading comprehension: A systematic meta-analytic review. *Educational Research Review, 30*, 100323.

Hoover, W. A., & Tunmer, W. E. (2018). The simple view of reading: Three assessments of its adequacy. *Remedial and Special Education, 39*(5), 304–312.

Hsu, Y. (2020). Teaching geometrics to young learners using computer-based simulation: The interaction effect of guidance, in relation to representation and manipulation, with socio-cultural background. *Interactive Learning Environments, 31*(1), 282–298.

Huttenlocher, J., Vasilyeva, M., Cymerman, E., & Levine, S. (2002). Language input and child syntax. *Cognitive Psychology, 45*(3), 337–374.

Huttenlocher, J., Vasilyeva, M., & Shimpi, P. (2004). Syntactic priming in young children. *Journal of Memory and Language, 50*(2), 182–195.

Hwang, H., & Cabell, S. Q. (2021). Latent profiles of vocabulary and domain knowledge and their relation to listening comprehension in kindergarten. *Journal of Research in Reading, 44*(3), 636–653.

Hwang, H., Cabell, S. Q., & Joyner, R. E. (2022). Effects of integrated literacy and content-area instruction on vocabulary and comprehension in the elementary years: A meta-analysis. *Scientific Studies of Reading, 26*(3), 223–249.

Hwang, H., Cabell, S. Q., & Joyner, R. E. (2023). Does cultivating content knowledge during literacy instruction support vocabulary and comprehension in the elementary school years? A systematic review. *Reading Psychology, 44*(2), 145–174.

Hwang, H., Lupo, S. M., Cabell, S. Q., & Wang, S. (2021). What research says about leveraging the literacy block for learning. *Reading in Virginia, 42*, 35–48.

Jacoby, N., & Fedorenko, E. (2020). Discourse-level comprehension engages medial frontal theory of mind brain regions even for expository texts. *Language, Cognition and Neuroscience, 35*(6), 780–796.

Jirout, J. J. (2020). Supporting early scientific thinking through curiosity. *Frontiers in Psychology, 11*.

Justice, L. M., Jiang, H., & Strasser, K. (2018). Linguistic environment of preschool classrooms: What dimensions support children's language growth? *Early Childhood Research Quarterly, 42*, 79–92.

Justice, L. M., McGinty, A. S., Zucker, T., Cabell, S. Q., & Piasta, S. B. (2013). Bi-directional dynamics underlie the complexity of talk in teacher-child play-based conversations in classrooms serving at-risk pupils. *Early Childhood Research Quarterly, 28*(3), 496–508.

Kieffer, M. J., & Lesaux, N. K. (2010). Morphing into adolescents: Active word learning for English-language learners and their classmates in Middle School. *Journal of Adolescent & Adult Literacy, 54*(1), 47–56.

Kiernan, B., & Gray, S. (1998). Word learning in a supported-learning context by preschool children with specific language impairment. *Journal of Speech, Language, and Hearing Research, 41*(1), 161–171.

Kim, J. S., & Burkhauser, M. A. (2022). Teaching for transfer can help young children read for understanding. *Phi Delta Kappan, 103*(8), 20–24.

Kim, J. S., Burkhauser, M. A., Relyea, J. E., Gilbert, J. B., Scherer, E., Fitzgerald, J., Mosher, D., & McIntyre, J. (2023). A longitudinal randomized trial of a sustained content literacy intervention from first to second grade: Transfer effects on students' reading comprehension. *Journal of Educational Psychology, 115*(1), 73–98.

Kim, J. S., Gilbert, J. B., Relyea, J. E., Rich, P., Scherer, E., Burkhauser, M. A., & Tvedt, J. N. (2023). *Time to transfer: Long-term effects of a sustained and spiraled content literacy intervention in the elementary grades.* EdWorkingPaper: 23–769.

Kintsch, E. (2005). Comprehension theory as a guide for the design of thoughtful questions. *Topics in Language Disorders, 25*(1), 51–64.

Kintsch, W. (1998). *Comprehension: A paradigm for cognition.* Cambridge University Press.

Kotaman, H., & Tekin, A. K. (2017). Informational and fictional books: Young children's book preferences and teachers' perspectives. *Early Child Development and Care, 187*(3–4), 600–614.

Kurkul, K. E., Dwyer, J., & Corriveau, K. H. (2022). "What do YOU think?": Children's questions, teacher's responses and children's follow-up across diverse preschool settings. *Early Childhood Research Quarterly, 58*, 231–241.

Landry, S. H., Smith, K. E., & Swank, P. R. (2006). Responsive parenting: Establishing early foundations for social, communication, and independent problem-solving skills. *Developmental Psychology, 42*(4), 627–642.

Landry, S. H., Zucker, T. A., Montroy, J. J., Hsu, H. Y., Assel, M. A., Varghese, C., Crawford, A., & Feil, E. G. (2021). Replication of combined school readiness interventions for teachers and parents of Head Start pre-kindergarteners using remote delivery. *Early Childhood Research Quarterly, 56*, 149–166.

Landry, S. H., Zucker, T. A., Williams, J. M., Merz, E. C., Guttentag, C. L., & Taylor, H. B. (2017). Improving school readiness of high-risk preschoolers: Combining high quality instructional strategies with responsive training for teachers and parents. *Early Childhood Research Quarterly, 40*, 38–51.

Language and Reading Research Consortium (LARRC). (2015). Learning to read: Should we keep things simple? *Reading Research Quarterly, 50*(2), 151–169.

Larson, A. L., Cycyk, L. M., Carta, J. J., Hammer, C. S., Baralt, M., Uchikoshi, Y., An, Z. G., & Wood, C. (2020). A systematic review of language-focused interventions for young children from culturally and linguistically diverse backgrounds. *Early Childhood Research Quarterly, 50*, 157–178.

Leech, K., Wei, R., Harring, J. R., & Rowe, M. L. (2018). A brief parent-focused intervention to improve preschoolers' conversational skills and school readiness. *Developmental Psychology, 54*(1), 15–28.

Lillard, A. S., Lerner, M. D., Hopkins, E. J., Dore, R. A., Smith, E. D., & Palmquist, C. M. (2013). The impact of pretend play on children's development: A review of the evidence. *Psychological Bulletin, 139*(1), 1–34.

Logan, J. A., Justice, L. M., Yumuş, M., & Chaparro-Moreno, L. J. (2019). When children are not read to at home: The million word gap. *Journal of Developmental & Behavioral Pediatrics, 40*(5), 383–386.

López, A., Najafi, B., Rogoff, B., & Mejía-Arauz, R. (2012). Collaboration and helping as cultural practices. *Oxford Handbooks Online.*

MacKay, K. L., Young, T. A., Munóz, S. H., & Motzkus, T. L. (2020). Expository texts in first-grade classroom libraries: Issues in teacher selection. *Reading Psychology*, 1–23.

Maloch, B., & Bomer, R. (2013). Informational texts and the common core standards: What are we talking about, anyway? *Language Arts, 90*(3), 205.

Mancilla-Martinez, J., & Lesaux, N. K. (2010). Predictors of reading comprehension for struggling readers: The case of Spanish-speaking language minority learners. *Journal of Educational Psychology, 102*(3), 701–711.

Mancilla-Martinez, J., Hwang, J. K., Oh, M. H., & Pokowitz, E. L. (2020). Patterns of development in Spanish–English conceptually scored vocabulary among elementary-age dual language learners. *Journal of Speech, Language, and Hearing Research, 63*(9), 3084–3099.

Mapp, K., Carver, I., & Lander, J. (2017). *Powerful partnerships: A teacher's guide to engaging families for student success.* Scholastic.

McDaniel, B. T. (2019). Parent distraction with phones, reasons for use, and impacts on parenting and child outcomes: A review of the emerging research. *Human Behavior and Emerging Technologies, 1*(2), 72–80.

McMaster, K. L., Kung, S.-H., Han, I., & Cao, M. (2008). Peer-Assisted Learning Strategies: A "tier 1" approach to promoting English learners' response to intervention. *Exceptional Children, 74*(2), 194–214.

McWayne, C., Foster, B., & Melzi, G. (2018). Culturally embedded measurement of Latino caregivers' engagement in Head Start: A tale of two forms of engagement. *Early Education and Development, 29*(4), 540–562.

Mejía-Arauz, R., Roberts, A. D., & Rogoff, B. (2012). Cultural variation in balance of nonverbal conversation and talk. *International Perspectives in Psychology, 1*(4), 207–220.

Metsala, J. L., & Walley, A. C. (1998). Spoken vocabulary growth and the segmental restructuring of lexical representations: Precursors to phonemic awareness and early reading ability. In J.L. Metsala & L.C. Ehri (Eds.), *Word recognition in beginning literacy* (pp. 89–120). Lawrence Erlbaum Associates.

Meyer, B. J., & Wijekumar, K. (2007). A web-based tutoring system for the structure strategy: Theoretical background, design, and findings. *Reading comprehension strategies: Theories, interventions, and technologies* (pp. 347–375). Lawrence Erlbaum Associates.

Mol, S. E., Bus, A. G., & de Jong, M. T. (2009). Interactive book reading in early education: A tool to stimulate print knowledge as well as oral language. *American Educational Research Journal, 79*(2), 979–1007.

Molinari, L., Mameli, C., & Gnisci, A. (2013). A sequential analysis of classroom discourse in Italian primary schools: The many faces of the IRF pattern. *British Journal of Educational Psychology, 83*(3), 414–430.

Myhill, D., & Warren, P. (2005). Scaffolds or straitjackets? Critical moments in classroom discourse. *Educational Review, 57*(1), 55–69.

National Academies of Sciences, Engineering, and Medicine. (2015). *Transforming the workforce for children birth through age 8: A unifying foundation.* The National Academies Press.

National Academies of Sciences, Engineering, and Medicine. (2017). *Promoting the educational success of children and youth learning English: Promising futures.* The National Academies Press.

National Early Literacy Panel (US). (2008). *Developing early literacy: Report of the National Early Literacy Panel: A scientific synthesis of early literacy development and implications for intervention.* National Institute for Literacy.

National Governors Association. (2010). *Common core state standards.*

National Institute of Child Health and Human Development, NIH, DHHS. (2010). *Developing Early Literacy: Report of the National Early Literacy Panel (NA).* U.S. Government Printing Office.

National Research Council. (2012). *A framework for K–12 science education: Practices, crosscutting concepts, and core ideas.* The National Academies Press.

Nelson, K. E., Camarata, S. M., Welsh, J., Butkovsky, L., & Camarata, M. (1996). Effects of imitative and conversational recasting treatment on the acquisition of grammar in children with specific language impairment and younger language-normal children. *Journal of Speech, Language, and Hearing Research, 39*(4), 850–859.

Neuman, S. B. (2006). The knowledge gap: Implications for early education. *Handbook of early literacy research, 2*, 29–40.

Neuman, S. B., & Kaefer, T. (2018b). Developing low-income children's vocabulary and content knowledge through a shared book reading program. *Contemporary Educational Psychology, 52*, 15–24.

Neuman, S. B., Kaefer, T., & Pinkham, A. M. (2018a). A double dose of disadvantage: Language experiences for low-income children in home and school. *Journal of Educational Psychology, 110*(1), 102.

Neuman, S. B., & Knapczyk, J. (2022). Early literacy in everyday settings: Creating an opportunity to learn for low-income young children. *Reading Research Quarterly, 57*(4), 1167–1186.

Neuman, S. B., Newman, E. H., & Dwyer, J. (2011). Educational effects of a vocabulary intervention on preschoolers' word knowledge and conceptual development: A cluster-randomized trial. *Reading Research Quarterly, 46*(3), 249–272.

Neuman, S. B., & Roskos, K. (1993). Access to print for children of poverty: Differential effects of adult mediation and literacy-enriched play settings on environmental and functional print tasks. *American Educational Research Journal, 30*(1), 95–122.

Neuman, S. B., Samudra, P., & Danielson, K. (2021). Effectiveness of scaling up a vocabulary intervention for low-income children, pre-K through first grade. *The Elementary School Journal, 121*(3), 385–409.

Orcutt, E., Johnson, V., & Kendeou, P. (2023). Comprehension: From language to reading. In S. Q. Cabell, S. B. Neuman, & N. Patton Terry (Eds.), *Handbook on the science of early literacy* (pp. 196–207). Guilford.

Paige, D. D., Wong Fillmore, L., Cabell, S., Goldenberg, C., & Griffin, A. (2021). *Comparing reading research to program design: An examination of McGraw Hill Education's Wonders, an elementary literacy curriculum.* Achieve the Core.

Pappas, C. C. (2006). The information book genre: Its role in integrated science literacy research and practice. *Reading Research Quarterly, 41*(2), 226–250.

Paul, R. (1995). *Language disorders from infancy through adolescence: Assessment and intervention.* Mosby-Year Book.

Pence, K. L., Justice, L. M., & Wiggins, A. K. (2008). Preschool teachers' fidelity in implementing a comprehensive language-rich curriculum. *Language, Speech, and Hearing Services in Schools, 39*(3), 329–341.

Pentimonti, J. M., & Justice, L. M. (2010). Teachers' use of scaffolding strategies during read alouds in the preschool classroom. *Early Childhood Education Journal, 37*(4), 241–248.

Pentimonti, J. M., Zucker, T. A., & Justice, L. M. (2011). What are preschool teachers reading in their classrooms? *Reading Psychology, 32*(3), 197–236.

Pentimonti, J. M., Zucker, T. A., Justice, L. M., & Kaderavek, J. N. (2010). Informational text use in preschool classroom read-alouds. *The Reading Teacher, 63*(8), 656–665.

Pérez, A. M., Peña, E. D., & Bedore, L. M. (2010). Cognates facilitate word recognition in young Spanish-English bilinguals' test performance. *Early Childhood Services, 4*(1), 55.

Perfetti, C. (2007). Reading ability: Lexical quality to comprehension. *Scientific Studies of Reading, 11*(4), 357–383.

Petscher, Y., Cabell, S., Catts, H. W., Compton, D., Foorman, B., Hart, S. A., Lonigan, C., Phillips, B., Schatschneider, C., Steacy, L. M., Terry, N. P., & Wagner, R. (2020). How the science of reading informs 21st century education. *Reading Research Quarterly, 55*(S1), S267–S282.

Petscher, Y., Justice, L. M., & Hogan, T. (2018). Modeling the early language trajectory of language development when the measures change and its relation to poor reading comprehension. *Child Development, 89*(6), 2136–2156.

Pillinger, C., & Vardy, E. J. (2022). The story so far: A systematic review of the dialogic reading literature. *Journal of Research in Reading, 45*(4), 533–548.

Pollard-Durodola, S. D., & Simmons, D. C. (2009). The role of explicit instruction and instructional design in promoting phonemic awareness development and transfer from Spanish to English. *Reading and Writing Quarterly, 25*(2–3), 139–161.

Pollard-Durodola, S. D., Gonzalez, J. E., Saenz, L., Soares, D., Davis, H. S., Resendez, N., & Zhu, L. (2022). The social validity of content enriched shared book reading vocabulary instruction and preschool DLL's language outcomes. *Early Education and Development, 33*(7), 1175–1197.

Pollard-Durodola, S. D., Gonzalez, J. E., Saenz, L., Soares, D., Resendez, N., Kwok, O., Davis, H., & Zhu, L. (2016). The effects of content-related shared book reading on the language development of preschool dual language learners. *Early Childhood Research Quarterly, 36*, 106–121.

Poventud, L. S., Corbett, N. L., Daunic, A. P., Aydin, B., Lane, H., & Smith, S. W. (2015). Developing social-emotional vocabulary to support self-regulation for young children at risk for emotional and behavioral problems. *International Journal of School and Cognitive Psychology, 2*(143), 2.

Price, L. H., Bradley, B. A., & Smith, J. M. (2012). A comparison of preschool teachers' talk during storybook and information book read-alouds. *Early Childhood Research Quarterly, 27*(3), 426–440.

Proctor, C. P., Silverman, R. D., Harring, J. R., Jones, R. L., & Hartranft, A. M. (2020). Teaching bilingual learners: Effects of a language-based reading intervention on academic language and reading comprehension in grades 4 and 5. *Reading Research Quarterly, 55*(1), 95–122.

Pullen, P. C., Tuckwiller, E. D., Konold, T. R., Maynard, K. L., & Coyne, M. D. (2010). A tiered intervention model for early vocabulary instruction: The effects of tiered instruction for young students at risk for reading disability. *Learning Disabilities Research and Practice, 25*(3), 110–123.

Quinn, S., Donnelly, S., & Kidd, E. (2018). The relationship between symbolic play and language acquisition: A meta-analytic review. *Developmental Review, 49*, 121–135.

Ramsook, K. A., Welsh, J. A., & Bierman, K. L. (2020). What you say, and how you say it: Preschoolers' growth in vocabulary and communication skills differentially predict kindergarten academic achievement and self-regulation. *Social Development, 29*(3), 783–800.

Ricketts, J., Nation, K., & Bishop, D. V. (2007). Vocabulary is important for some, but not all reading skills. *Scientific Studies of Reading, 11*(3), 235–257.

Roberts, T. A. (2008). Home storybook reading in primary or second language with preschool children: Evidence of equal effectiveness for second-language vocabulary acquisition. *Reading Research Quarterly, 43*(2), 103–130.

Rogoff, B., Mejía-Arauz, R., & Correa-Chávez, M. (2015). A cultural paradigm—learning by observing and pitching in. *Advances in Child Development and Behavior*, 1–22.

Romeo, R. R., Leonard, J. A., Robinson, S. T., West, M. R., Mackey, A. P., Rowe, M. L., & Gabrieli, J. D. (2018). Beyond the 30-million-word gap: Children's conversational exposure is associated with language-related brain function. *Psychological Science, 29*(5), 700–710.

Roskos, K., & Christie, J. (2001). Examining the play–literacy interface: A critical review and future directions. *Journal of Early Childhood Literacy, 1*(1), 59–89.

Rowe, M. L. (2012). A longitudinal investigation of the role of quantity and quality of child-directed speech in vocabulary development. *Child Development, 83*(5), 1762–1774.

Rowe, M. L., Romeo, R. R., & Leech, K. A. (2023). Early environmental influences on language. In S. Q. Cabell, S. B. Neuman, and N. Patton Terry (Eds.), *Handbook on the science of early literacy* (pp. 23–31). Guilford.

Scarborough, H. (2001). Connecting early language and literacy to later reading (dis) abilities: evidence, theory and practice. In S. B. Neuman & D. K. Dickinson (Eds.), *Handbook of early literacy research* (Vol. 1, pp. 97–110). Guilford.

Scholastic Inc. (2019). *Kids and family reading report: 7th edition.* Scholastic. https://www.scholastic.com/content/dam/KFRR/Downloads/KFRRReport_Finding%20Their%20Story.pdf

Sedova, K., Sedlacek, M., Svaricek, R., Majcik, M., Navratilova, J., Drexlerova, A., Kychler, J., & Salamounova, Z. (2019). Do those who talk more learn more? The relationship between student classroom talk and student achievement. *Learning and Instruction, 63*, 101217.

Sénéchal, M. (1997). The differential effect of storybook reading on preschoolers' acquisition of expressive and receptive vocabulary. *Journal of Child Language, 24*(1), 123–138.

Serpell, R., Sonnenschein, S., Baker, L., & Ganapathy, H. (2002). Intimate culture of families in the early socialization of literacy. *Journal of Family Psychology, 16*(4), 391–405.

Shanahan, T. (2020). What constitutes a science of reading instruction? *Reading Research Quarterly, 55*(S1).

Sharma, S., Chuang, R.-J., & Hedberg, A. M. (2011). Pilot-testing CATCH early childhood. *American Journal of Health Education, 42*(1), 12–23.

Shavlik, M., Köksal, Ö., French, B. F., Haden, C. A., Legare, C. H., & Booth, A. E. (2022). Contributions of causal reasoning to early scientific literacy. *Journal of Experimental Child Psychology, 224*, 105509.

Sheridan, S. M., Koziol, N., Witte, A. L., Iruka, I., & Knoche, L. L. (2020). Longitudinal and geographic trends in family engagement during the pre-kindergarten to kindergarten transition. *Early Childhood Education Journal, 48*(3), 365–377.

Silva, K. G., Shimpi, P. M., & Rogoff, B. (2015). Young children's attention to what's going on. *Advances in Child Development and Behavior*, 207–227.

Silverman, R. D. (2007). Vocabulary development of English-language and English-only learners in kindergarten. *The Elementary School Journal, 107*(4), 365–383.

Silverman, R., & Hines, S. (2009). The effects of multimedia-enhanced instruction on the vocabulary of English-language learners and non-English-language learners in pre-kindergarten through second grade. *Journal of Educational Psychology, 101*(2), 305–314.

Silverman, R. D., Johnson, E., Keane, K., & Khanna, S. (2020). Beyond decoding: A meta-analysis of the effects of language comprehension interventions on K–5 students' language and literacy outcomes. *Reading Research Quarterly, 55*, (S207–S233).

Silverman, R., Kim, Y.-S., Hartranft, A., Nunn, S., & McNeish, D. (2016). Effects of a multimedia enhanced reading buddies program on kindergarten and Grade 4 vocabulary and comprehension. *The Journal of Educational Research, 110*(4), 391–404.

Silverman, R. D., Proctor, C. P., Harring, J. R., Doyle, B., Mitchell, M. A., & Meyer, A. G. (2014). Teachers' instruction and students' vocabulary and comprehension: An exploratory study with English monolingual and Spanish-English bilingual students in grades 3-5. *Reading Research Quarterly, 49*(1), 31–60.

Simons, C., Sonnenschein, S., Sawyer, B., Kong, P., & Brock, A. (2021). School readiness beliefs of Dominican and Salvadoran immigrant parents. *Early Education and Development, 33*(2), 268–289.

Smith, S. A., Carlo, M. S., Park, S., & Kaplan, H. (2023). Exploring the promise of augmented reality for dual-language vocabulary learning among bilingual children. *CALICO Journal, 40*(1).

Snow, C. E. (1991). The theoretical basis for relationships between language and literacy in development. *Journal of Research in Childhood Education, 6*(1), 5–10.

Snow, C. E., & Kim, Y. S. (2007). Large problem spaces: The challenge of vocabulary for English language learners. In R. K. Wagner, A. E. Muse, & K. R. Tannenbaum (Eds.), *Vocabulary acquisition: Implications for reading comprehension* (pp. 123–139). Guilford.

Snowling, M. J., & Hulme, C. (2021). Annual research review: Reading disorders revisited—the critical importance of oral language. *Journal of Child Psychology and Psychiatry, 62*(5), 635–653.

Sobel, D. M., & Kirkham, N. Z. (2006). Blickets and babies: The development of causal reasoning in toddlers and infants. *Developmental Psychology, 42*(6), 1103–1115.

Solari, E. J., Denton, C. A., Petscher, Y., & Haring, C. (2018). Examining the effects and feasibility of a teacher-implemented tier 1 and tier 2 intervention in word reading, fluency, and comprehension. *Journal of Research on Educational Effectiveness, 11*(2), 163–191.

Solari, E. J., Kehoe, K. F., Cho, E., Hall, C., Vargas, I., Dahl-Leonard, K., Richmond, C. L., Henry, A. R., Cook, L., Hayes, L., & Conner, C. (2022). Effectiveness of interventions for English learners with word reading difficulties: A research synthesis. *Learning Disabilities Research Practice, 37*(3), 158–174.

Spencer, T. D., Petersen, D. B., & Adams, J. L. (2015). Tier 2 language intervention for diverse preschoolers: An early-stage randomized control group study following an analysis of response to intervention. *American Journal of Speech-Language Pathology, 24*(4), 619–636.

Squires, L. R., Ohlfest, S. J., Santoro, K. E., & Roberts, J. L. (2020). Factors influencing cognate performance for young multilingual children's vocabulary: A research synthesis. *American Journal of Speech-Language Pathology, 29*(4), 2170–2188.

Stafura, J. Z., & Perfetti, C. A. (2017). Integrating word processing with text comprehension. *Studies in Written Language and Literacy* (pp. 9–32).

Stanton-Chapman, T. L. (2015). Promoting positive peer interactions in the preschool classroom: The role and the responsibility of the teacher in supporting children's sociodramatic play. *Early Childhood Education Journal, 43*(2), 99–107.

Storch, S. A., & Whitehurst, G. J. (2002). Oral language and code-related precursors to reading: Evidence from a longitudinal structural model. *Developmental Psychology, 38*(6), 934–947.

Strommen, L. T., & Mates, B. F. (2004). Learning to love reading: Interviews with older children and teens. *Journal of Adolescent and Adult Literacy, 48*(3), 188–200.

Student Achievement Partners. (2021). *Achieve the Core offers free tools and resources to support grade-level, relevant, and joyful classroom learning.* Achieve the Core.

Suskind, D. L., Leffel, K. R., Graf, E., Hernandez, M. W., Gunderson, E. A., Sapolich, S. G., Suskind, E., Leininger, L., Goldin-Meadow, S., & Levine, S. C. (2015). A parent-directed language intervention for children of low socioeconomic status: A randomized controlled pilot study. *Journal of Child Language, 43*(2), 366–406.

Terry, N. P., Gatlin, B., & Johnson, L. (2018). Same or different: How bilingual readers can help us understand bidialectal readers. *Topics in Language Disorders, 38*, 50–65.

Tyner, A., & Kabourek, S. (2021). *How social studies improves elementary literacy.* National Council for the Social Studies.

U.S. Department of Education, Institute of Education Sciences, National Center for Education Statistics, National Assessment of Educational Progress (NAEP), (2022). Reading Assessments.

Vadasy, P. F., Sanders, E. A., & Nelson, J. R. (2015). Effectiveness of supplemental kindergarten vocabulary instruction for English learners: A randomized study of immediate and longer-term effects of two approaches. *Journal of Research on Educational Effectiveness, 8*(4), 490–529.

van den Noort, M., Struys, E., Bosch, P., Jaswetz, L., Perriard, B., Yeo, S., ... & Lim, S. (2019). Does the bilingual advantage in cognitive control exist and if so, what are its modulating factors? A systematic review. *Behavioral Sciences, 9*(3), 27.

van Kleeck, A., Stahl, S. A., & Bauer, E. B. (2003). Reading aloud to young children as a classroom instructional activity: Insights from research and practice. *On Reading Books to Children*, 123–147.

van Kleeck, A., Vander Woude, J., & Hammett, L. (2006). Fostering literal and inferential language skills in Head Start preschoolers with language impairment using scripted book-sharing discussions. *American Journal of Speech-Language Pathology, 15*(1), 85–95. Routledge.

Vartiainen, J., & Kumpulainen, K. (2020). Playing with science: Manifestation of scientific play in early science inquiry. *European Early Childhood Education Research Journal, 28*(4), 490–503.

Vitale, M. R., & Romance, N. R. (2012). Using in-depth science instruction to accelerate student achievement in science and reading comprehension in grades 1–2. *International Journal of Science and Mathematics Education, 10*, 457–472.

Vygotsky, L. S. (1978). *Mind in society: Development of higher psychological processes.* Harvard University Press.

Wang, S., Cabell, S., Hadley, E. B., Leushuis, A., Pentimonti, J. (2023).The frequency of informational text read-alouds in kindergarten classrooms and its association with students' vocabulary and knowledge development. [Manuscript submitted for publication]

Washington, J. A., & Seidenberg, M. S. (2021, Summer). Teaching reading to African American children: When home and school language differ. *American Educator, 45*(2), 26.

Wasik, B. A., & Hindman, A. H. (2011a). Factors contributing to high quality effective preschool interventions. In S. B. Neuman & D. K. Dickinson (Eds.), *Handbook of early literacy research* (Volume 3). Guilford.

Wasik, B. A., & Hindman, A. H. (2011b). Improving vocabulary and pre-literacy skills of at-risk preschoolers through teacher professional development. *Journal of Educational Psychology, 103*(2), 455–469.

Wasik, B. A., & Hindman, A. H. (2023). Story talk: Using strategies from an evidence-based program to improve young children's vocabulary. *The Reading Teacher, 76*(4), 429–438.

Wasik, B. A., Farrow, J., & Hindman, A. H. (2022). More than "good job!": The critical role of teacher feedback in classroom discourse and language development. *The Reading Teacher, 75*(6), 733–738.

Weisberg, D. S., Hirsh-Pasek, K., Golinkoff, R. M., Kittredge, A. K., & Klahr, D. (2016). Guided play: Principles and practices. *Current Directions in Psychological Science, 25*(3), 177–182.

Whitehurst, G. J., & Lonigan, C. J. (1998). Child development and emergent literacy. *Child Development, 69*(3), 848–872.

Whitehurst, G. J., Arnold, D. S., Epstein, J. N., Angell, A. L., Smith, M., & Fischel, J. E. (1994). A picture book reading intervention in day care and home for children from low-income families. *Developmental Psychology, 30*(5), 679–689.

Wijekumar, K., Meyer, B. J., Lei, P., Beerwinkle, A. L., & Joshi, M. (2020). Supplementing teacher knowledge using web-based intelligent tutoring system for the text structure strategy to improve content area reading comprehension with fourth- and fifth-grade struggling readers. *Dyslexia, 26*(2), 120–136.

Willingham, D. T. (2006). How knowledge helps: It speeds and strengthens reading comprehension, learning—and thinking. *American Educator, 30*, 1–12.

Wolfram, W., & Schilling-Estes, N. (2006). *American English: Dialects and variation* (2nd ed.). Blackwell.

Worthy, J., Durán, L., Hikida, M., Pruitt, A., & Peterson, K. (2013). Spaces for dynamic bilingualism in read-aloud discussions: Developing and strengthening bilingual and academic skills. *Bilingual Research Journal, 36*(3), 311–328.

Wright, T. S., & Neuman, S. B. (2013). Vocabulary instruction in commonly used kindergarten core reading curricula. *The Elementary School Journal, 113*(3), 386–408.

Wright, T. S., Cervetti, G. N., Wise, C., & McClung, N. A. (2022). The impact of knowledge-building through conceptually-coherent read alouds on vocabulary and comprehension. *Reading Psychology, 43*(1), 70–84.

Yopp, R. H., & Yopp, H. K. (2006). Informational texts as read-alouds at school and home. *Journal of Literacy Research, 38*(1), 37–51.

York, B. N., Loeb, S., & Doss, C. (2019). One step at a time. *Journal of Human Resources, 54*(3), 537–566.

Zucker, T. A., Bowles, R., Pentimonti, J., & Tambyraja, S. (2021). Profiles of teacher & child talk during early childhood classroom shared book reading. *Early Childhood Research Quarterly, 56*, 27–40.

Zucker, T. A., Cabell, S. Q., & Pico, D. L. (2021). Going nuts for words: Recommendations for teaching young students academic vocabulary. *The Reading Teacher, 74*(5), 581–594.

Zucker, T. A., Cabell, S. Q., Justice, L. M., Pentimonti, J. M., & Kaderavek, J. N. (2013). The role of frequent, interactive prekindergarten shared reading in the longitudinal development of language and literacy skills. *Developmental Psychology, 49*(8), 1425–1439.

Zucker, T. A., Cabell, S. Q., Oh, Y., & Wang, X. (2020). Asking questions is just the first step: Using upward and downward scaffolds. *The Reading Teacher, 74*(3), 275–283.

Zucker, T. A., Cabell, S. Q., Petscher, Y., Mui, H., Landry, S. H., & Tock, J. (2021). Teaching together: Pilot study of a tiered language and literacy intervention with Head Start teachers and linguistically diverse families. *Early Childhood Research Quarterly, 54*, 136–152

Zucker, T. A., Carlo, M. S., Landry, S. H., Masood-Saleem, S. S., Williams, J. M., & Bhavsar, V. (2019). Iterative design and pilot testing of the developing talkers tiered academic language curriculum for pre-kindergarten and kindergarten. *Journal of Research on Educational Effectiveness, 12*(2), 274–306.

Zucker, T. A., Carlo, M. S., Montroy, J. J., & Landry, S. H. (2021). Pilot test of the Hablemos Juntos tier 2 academic language curriculum for Spanish-speaking preschoolers. *Early Childhood Research Quarterly, 55*, 179–192.

Zucker, T. A., Jacbos, E., & Cabell, S. Q. (2021). Exploring barriers to early childhood teachers' implementation of a supplemental academic language curriculum. *Early Education and Development, 32*(8), 1194–1219.

Zucker, T. A., Justice, L. M., & Piasta, S. B. (2009). Prekindergarten teachers' verbal references to print during classroom-based, large-group shared reading. *Language, Speech, and Hearing Services in Schools, 40*(4), 376–392.

Zucker, T. A., Justice, L. M., Piasta, S. B., & Kaderavek, J. N. (2010). Preschool teachers' literal and inferential questions and children's responses during whole-class shared reading. *Early Childhood Research Quarterly, 25*(1), 65–83.

Zucker, T. A., Mesa, M. P., Logan, J., Assel, M., Oh, Y. (March, 2023). *Relations between frequency of early childhood teachers' vocabulary instruction and their own vocabulary, executive function and stress.* [Paper presentation]. Society for Research in Child Development, Biannual Conference, Salt Lake City, Utah.

Zucker, T. A., Solari, E. J., Landry, S. H., & Swank, P. R. (2013). Effects of a brief tiered language intervention for prekindergartners at risk. *Early Education and Development, 24*(3), 366–392.

Zucker, T. A., Yeomans-Maldonado, G., Surrain, S., & Landry, S. H. (2023). Together we can do so much. *Handbook on the Science of Early Literacy*, 269.

Index